WARRIOR 175

ROMAN LEGIONARY AD 284–337

The age of Diocletian and Constantine

ROSS COWAN

ILLUSTRATED BY SEÁN Ó'BRÓGÁIN

Series editor Marcus Cowper

OSPREY PUBLISHING
Bloomsbury Publishing Plc

Kemp House, Chawley Park, Cumnor Hill, Oxford OX2 9PH, UK
29 Earlsfort Terrace, Dublin 2, Ireland
1385 Broadway, 5th Floor, New York, NY 10018, USA
Email: info@ospreypublishing.com
www.ospreypublishing.com

OSPREY is a trademark of Osprey Publishing Ltd

First published in Great Britain in 2015

A CIP catalogue record for this book is available from the British Library.

Print ISBN: 978 1 4728 0666 6
ePub: 978 1 4728 0668 0
ePDF: 978 1 4728 0667 3

Editorial by Ilios Publishing Ltd, Oxford, UK (www.iliospublishing.com)
Artwork by Seán Ó'Brógáin
Index by Sharon Redmayne
Typeset in Myriad Pro and Sabon
Originated by PDQ Media, UK
Printed and bound in India by Replika Press Private Ltd.

22 23 24 25 26   10 9 8 7 6 5

The Woodland Trust

Osprey Publishing supports the Woodland Trust, the UK's leading woodland conservation charity.

www.ospreypublishing.com

To find out more about our authors and books visit our website. Here you will find extracts, author interviews, details of forthcoming events and the option to sign-up for our newsletter.

Acknowledgements

The author would like to thank all those who made photographs available. Special thanks to the Cowan family, Dr Duncan B. Campbell, Marcus Cowper, Dr Florian Himmler, Thomas McGrory, Seán Ó'Brógáin, Steven D. P. Richardson and Ian Ross.

Artist's note

Thanks to Legion Ireland (for the poses), Ben Kane, Tomas Brogan, John Callow and Graham Sumner. Readers may care to note that the original paintings from which the colour plates in this book were prepared are available for private sale. The Publishers retain all reproduction copyright whatsoever. All enquiries should be addressed to:

Seán Ó'Brógáin
Stragally
Commeen (R253)
Cloghan
Lifford
Donegal
Ireland

The Publishers regret that they can enter into no correspondence upon this matter.

CONTENTS

INTRODUCTION   4

CHRONOLOGY   4

RECRUITMENT AND TERMS OF SERVICE   8

BELIEF AND BELONGING   20

TRAINING   26

EQUIPMENT   31

ORGANIZATION AND COMMAND OF THE LEGION   33

ON CAMPAIGN   39

BATTLE   55

AFTER THE BATTLE   57

FURTHER READING   60

GLOSSARY   62

INDEX   64

ROMAN LEGIONARY AD 284–337

INTRODUCTION

Diocletian and Constantine were the greatest of the later Roman emperors, and their era marks the climax of the traditional legionary system – Diocletian created more legions than any emperor since Augustus. Most frontier provinces were defended by a pair of legions, and field armies were composed of detachments drawn from those legions. Diocletian thus continued a centuries-old practice. However, he also began a process of dividing legions, including his new creations, into 'half-legions' and the detachments withdrawn for field army service, or garrison duties in foreign provinces, tended not to return to their parent formations. They became small, independent 'legions'. This ensured the permanent break-up of the classic Roman legion of ten cohorts, and those attached to the increasingly permanent imperial field armies achieved elite status and better terms of service, while the frontier legions were essentially downgraded. Constantine began the process of formalizing the division of the army into elite *comitatenses* (field army units) and *ripenses or limitanei* (river bank or frontier units) in AD 325. However, the fully developed Late Roman legion of the mid- and late 4th century AD lies beyond the scope of this book. The legionary forces of AD 284–337, organized in cohorts and centuries and led by prefects, *praepositi* and centurions, would have been recognizable to Roman generals of earlier eras, and legionaries continued to form the backbone of the army.

Diocletian depicted in the typical fashion of a 'soldier-emperor' of the late 3rd century AD, with radiate crown and a practical short, cropped hair. He is unshaven because he was continually on campaign or labouring on behalf of the Empire. The reverse celebrates 'the harmony of the army'. (© RHC Archive)

CHRONOLOGY

(All dates AD)

284	Assassination of Numerian; Diocles, commander of the *protectores*, is proclaimed emperor and takes the name Diocletian.
285	Carinus, brother and co-emperor of Numerian, defeats usurper Julianus at Verona but is in turn defeated by Diocletian at the Margus. Diocletian appoints Maximian Caesar (junior emperor); Maximian defeats the Bagaudae and repels German invasion of Gaul. Diocletian defeats the Sarmatians.
286	Maximian promoted to Augustus (senior emperor). Revolt of Carausius in Britain and northern Gaul.

Maximian. His loyalty to Diocletian was unswerving, but he chafed in retirement and tried to usurp Maxentius and then Constantine, who forced him to commit suicide. (© G. Dall'Orto)

286–287	German raids across the Rhine into Roman territory. Maximian leads major punitive expedition into Germany.
288	Frankish king Gennoboudes submits to Maximian.
289	Diocletian campaigns against the Sarmatians. Failure of Maximian's naval operations against Carausius.
290	Diocletian's second campaign against the Saracens.
293	Diocletian establishes the Tetrarchy with Constantius and Galerius as Caesars. Constantius captures Boulogne and ejects Carausius' forces from Gaul; Carausius assassinated and replaced by Allectus in Britain. Constantius defeats German invasion of Batavia. Revolt in Upper Egypt.

Constantine in AD 307/8. Charismatic and supremely ambitious, he fought three civil wars to bring the whole of the Roman Empire under his rule. (© RHC Archive)

294	Galerius defeats Egyptian rebels.
295	Galerius campaigns against the Persians.
296	Constantius and praetorian prefect Asclepiodotus recapture Britain. Maximian holds Rhine frontier and then campaigns in Spain. Diocletian defeats the Quadi, campaigns against the Carpi, and then conducts operations against Persia.
297	Maximian campaigns against Quinquegentiani in Mauretania. Galerius defeated by Narses I of Persia near Carrhae. Domitianus and Achilles revolt in Egypt.
297–298	Diocletian besieges Alexandria and defeats Egyptian rebels.
298	Maximian campaigns in Tripolitania. Galerius defeats Narses in Armenia and captures Ctesiphon.
299/300	Purge of Christians from the Roman Army. Galerius campaigns against the Marcomanni.
300/1	Constantius defeats the Franks.
301	Galerius campaigns against the Carpi.
302	Galerius fights the Carpi and Sarmatians.
302	Constantius defeats the Alamanni at Lingones.
303	Galerius campaigns against the Carpi. Constantius is victorious over the Germans at Vindonissa.
304	Constantius repels German raiders. Diocletian defeats the Carpi.
305	Abdication of Diocletian and Maximian; Constantius and Galerius become senior emperors with Severus and Maximinus as their Caesars; Constantius defeats the Picts.
306	Death of Constantius at York; his eldest son Constantine is declared emperor by the army in Britain. Maxentius is elevated by the Praetorian Guard in Rome and calls his father, Maximian, out of retirement.
306/7	Galerius achieves victories over the Sarmatians. Constantine fights the Franks.
307	Severus, official senior emperor in the West, marches on Rome to eject Maxentius, but his army deserts to Maximian; Severus is imprisoned and later executed. Galerius invades Italy and approaches Rome, but is forced to withdraw when his soldiers start to desert to Maxentius and Maximian.
308	Constantine attacks the Bructeri and bridges the Rhine at Cologne. Domitius Alexander revolts against Maxentius in Africa. Conference of official emperors at Carnuntum: Maximian compelled to retire again; Licinius made Augustus and charged with defeating Maxentius.
308–309	Galerius fights the Carpi. Licinius campaigns against Maxentius' forces in Dalmatia and north-east Italy.
309	Domitius Alexander is defeated by Maxentius' praetorian prefect, Volusianus.
310	Constantine campaigns against the Franks. Maximian revolts against Constantine but is defeated at Marseille and commits suicide. Maximinus campaigns on the

	Persian frontier. Licinius defeats the Sarmatians.
311	Death of Galerius. Maximinus attempts to seize Licinius' Asian provinces.
312	Constantine invades Italy, captures Segusium, and defeats Maxentius' armies at Turin, Brixia and Verona; Constantine advances on Rome; defeat and death of Maxentius at the Milvian Bridge. Maximinus campaigning in Armenia. Death of Diocletian.
313	Maximinus invades Thrace but is defeated by Licinius at Campus Ergenus; Maximinus commits suicide; Licinius secures his position by ordering the executions of the families of Diocletian, Galerius and Maximinus. Constantine campaigns on the Lower Rhine.
313/4	Licinius campaigns on the Persian frontier.
314	Constantine campaigning in Germany.
314/5	Licinius fights the Sarmatians.
316	Constantine defeats Licinius at Cibalae.
317	Licinius defeated at Adrianople but turns Constantine's position at Beroea and forces a negotiated settlement; he cedes his European territories, with the exception of the diocese of Thrace, to Constantine.
318	Licinius campaigns against the Sarmatians.
319	Crispus, son of Constantine, campaigns against the Franks.
323	Constantine defeats Sarmatian invaders at Campona, Margus and Bononia and pursues them across the Danube. Crispus campaigns on the Rhine.
324	Constantine defeats Gothic incursion. Licinius defeated at Adrianople and besieged in Byzantium by Constantine; Crispus defeats Licinius' fleet in the Hellespont; Constantine defeats Licinius and his Gothic allies at Chrysopolis; Licinius abdicates. Empire reunited under Constantine.
325	Licinius is accused of plotting against Constantine and executed.
326	Constantine executes Crispus (son by his first marriage) and Fausta (his second wife) following a mysterious scandal.
328	Constantine bridges the Danube at Oescus and defeats the Goths; he proceeds to campaign on the Rhine.
330	Constantinus, son of Constantine, campaigns against the Alamanni.
332	Constantine wins major Gothic victory.
334	Constantine campaigns against the Sarmatians.
336	Constantine campaigns north of the Danube and takes the title Dacicus Maximus to celebrate the reconquest of former Roman territory.
337	Constantine prepares for war with Persia but falls ill and dies at Nicomedia.

Maximentius was overlooked in the succession of AD 305, but in 306 he was elevated by the Praetorian Guard. He was the last emperor to rule from Rome. (© RHC Archive)

RECRUITMENT AND TERMS OF SERVICE

Age at recruitment

In our period, most recruits to the legions were aged between 16 and 20. Valerius Flavinus was 16 when he joined a detachment of *legio XI Claudia* at Aquileia in north-east Italy (*CIL* V 895). A certain Iulius (his *nomen*, or family name, is lost) and Aurelius Iustinus were approved for service (*probatus*) in the same legion when aged 16 and 17 respectively (*ILS* 2333, 2332). Their epitaphs render the term *probatus* into soldiers' speak as *probitus* or *provitus*. We occasionally come across even younger recruits, such as Florius Baudio, aged only 15 when he enrolled in *legio II Italica* in *c.* AD 282 (*ILS* 2777).

Valerius Saturnanus entered *II Italica* aged 17 (*CIL* XI 4085). He fought alongside Baudio in the *Divitenses* detachment of the legion during Constantine's invasion of Italy in AD 312 (below). An anonymous legionary joined *II Italica* when he was 18; he died seven years later in Maximian's African War of AD 297–8 (*AE* 1972, 709). Martinus, a Christian legionary, enrolled in the German legion, *I Minervia*, aged 19. He was later transferred to *XI Claudia*, then to the *lanciarii* and eventually became a *protector* (*ILS* 2782). Valerius Iustinus, another *II Italica* casualty of Constantine's Italian campaign, joined the legion aged 20 in AD 307 (*AE* 1982, 258).

Older recruits, or conscripts, in their mid-20s were not uncommon. Valerius Genialis, a standard-bearer of *legio II Italica*, probably died at, or shortly after, the battle of the Milvian Bridge in AD 312. He had been recruited 26 years earlier at the age of 24 (*ILS* 2346). Aurelius Saturninus, who entered *legio I Italica* at the age of 26, was evidently a brave man, for at some point before his death aged 40, he became *torquatus*, a legionary decorated with a neck torque for an exceptional act of valour (*AE* 1983, 59; Vegetius 2.7).

The gravestone of Aurelius Iustinus, who was recruited into *legio XI Claudia* at the age of 17. Originally an infantryman, he served in the century of a *hastatus posterior*. After six years he was promoted into the legion's *equites* (cavalry) (*ILS* 2332). (© Steven D. P. Richardson)

By simply subtracting his length of service (12 years) from his age at death (38), we might think that Claudius Iustinianus, a *centurio ordinarius* of *legio II Adiutrix* on detachment at Aquileia, was also recruited at the age of 26 (*ILS* 2408). However, Iustinianus' service is qualified by the term *salariorum*, meaning he received a special salary and not the usual *stipendium* (military pay) received by other centurions. It may be that his epitaph fails to mention previous military service undertaken before promotion to the senior centurionate.

Geographical origins

As in previous centuries, the legions gained the bulk of their recruits from local or regional sources, but drafts from further afield were not uncommon (e.g. *AE* 1975, 815, mentions a levy from Asia Minor for service in the Balkans).

Valerius Longinianus, a centurion of *legio XI Claudia* at Aquileia, was born in the fortress of Abritus (Razgrad) in Moesia Inferior and was presumably the son of a soldier. He would have enlisted at the headquarters of *XI Claudia* at Durostorum (Silistra) and was subsequently transferred to Italy. Longinianus' epitaph also reflects the way the soldiers at Aquileia spoke; Moesia is rendered 'Mensia' (*CIL* V 942). One would have expected Aurelius Maximianus, from a small village in the territory of Marcianopolis (Devnya), to have joined *XI Claudia*, his local legion, but instead he was recruited into *I Adiutrix*, which had its base hundreds of miles to the west in Pannonia. It may be that Maximianus was conscripted into *I Adiutrix* when a *vexillatio* (detachment) of the legion was present in Moesia during one of the Gothic, Carpic or Sarmatian wars of the late 3rd century AD. Like Longinianus, he ended his days serving in a vexillation at strategic Aquileia (*CIL* V 892).

Valerius Aulucentius, another centurion of *XI Claudia* at Aquileia, was, as his second name indicates, a Thracian (*CIL* V 940). The Roman provinces of Moesia, forming the eastern section of the Danube frontier, were established on old Thracian territories and the detachment of *XI Claudia* at Aquileia had a strong Thracian contingent. Aurelius Sudlecentius (*CIL* V 900) and Aurelius Dizo bear typical Thracian names. The latter was killed in Maximian's African War. When the vexillation returned to Aquileia in AD 299, a memorial was erected for Dizo by his 'fellow-citizens', meaning

Aurelius Sudlecentius, a Thracian legionary of *XI Claudia* at Aquileia (*CIL* V 900). He bears the typical fighting gear of a legionary: *scutum* (oval shield), a pair of *tela* (barbed javelins) and a *gladius* or *spatha* (cut-and-thrust sword). (© Steven D. P. Richardson)

Thracians, 'and fellow-soldiers', the non-Thracian legionaries (*CIL* V 893). Another Dizo of *XI Claudia* was commemorated at Concordia, a garrison city about 30 miles west of Aquileia (Pais 412).

The manpower of the detachments based at Aquileia was not drawn exclusively from the traditional recruiting grounds of the parent legions. Aurelius Flavinus, mentioned above, lacks a distinctive Thracian name and his epitaph fails to mention a place of origin. He was probably a local man (Adams & Brennan 1990, 185). Aquileia certainly provided recruits to the legions in our era. Valerius Ursianus, 'a citizen of Aquileia', was *provitus* at 18 and served in *legio X Gemina* for five years before winning a transfer to Maxentius' Praetorian Guard (*CIL* VI 37207). It seems likely that he did not enrol at the legion's headquarters at *Vindobona* (Vienna) in Pannonia, but joined the detachment based in his native city.

Aquileia had long been a garrison city. Strategically located between the head of the Adriatic and the foot of the Julian Alps, it controlled the main land route between Italy, Pannonia and Illyricum and access to the sea. Originally a base for Augustus' conquest of Illyricum, it became a major hub for trade and communications. After Milan, it served as Maximian's residence in Italy, but it was not necessarily a comfortable billet. The legionaries based at Aquileia might be called upon to hunt bandits in the Julian Alps (*Inscr. Aquil.* II 2785, for a centurion killed by bandits) or to defend the city and the surrounding region from the forces of rival emperors. It was on the front line in the conflict between Maxentius and Licinius (*ILS* 2776, a 50-year-old *protector* of Licinius' army 'killed in the civil war in Italy', *c.* AD 309), and finally fell by siege to Constantine in the war of AD 312 (*Latin Panegyrics* 12(9).11.1, 4(10).27.1).

Even in times of peace, mortality rates at Aquileia were high. Flavius Augustalis was part of the Constantinian garrison. He was a centurion of '*legio Prima Italica* of Moesia' and died aged 41 after 20 years and six months of service. His son, Stercorius, followed him to the Underworld 47 days later and they were commemorated on the same gravestone. The inscription records how many years, months, days and even hours father and son lived; the hours indicate the time of day at which they died (*CIL* V 914).

Soldiers might also be recruited from defeated barbarians settled within the Empire (*laeti*), or from peoples living adjacent to the frontiers. Florius Baudio's name suggests Germanic origin (*ILS* 2777). In the final civil war against Licinius (AD 324), one of Constantine's generals is identified as Bonitus, a Frank (Ammianus Marcellinus 15.5.33). It is possible that he rose through the ranks of the legions: he may be the same Bonitus who was *praepositus* of a detachment of *legio VII Claudia* in the early 4th century AD (*AE* 1910, 90; Barnes 2014, 155).

Social origins

The peasant, conservative, strong, hard-working and untainted by the pleasures of the city, was considered the ideal legionary recruit (cf. Vegetius 1.3). Aurelius Maximianus of *I Aditurix*, coming from a village in rural Moesia, was of such yeoman stock. Before joining the army, the future emperor Galerius was an *armentarius*, a cattle herder, in New Dacia (*Epitome de Caesaribus* 40.15). Galerius' preference for *V Macedonia* might suggest the emperor's military career began in that legion (Christodoulou 2002).

Maximian was born near Sirmium (Sremska Mitrovica) into a family of *agresti*, 'country dwellers', in *c.* AD 250 (*Epitome de Caesaribus* 40.10). He

may have begun his military career in one of the Pannonian legions. In AD 289, an orator sought to flatter the emperor by reminding him of his upbringing in Pannonia, 'the seat of the bravest legions' (*Latin Panegyrics* 10(2).2.4), but at the time of Maximian's youth, the nearest legionary base was that of *IIII Flavia* at Singidunum (Belgrade), across the provincial border in Moesia.

The sons of soldiers and veterans were expected to follow their fathers into the army. Thus Valerius Varius followed his father, Florius Baudio, into *legio II Italica Divitensium*, and progressed to at least the rank of *optio* (*ILS* 2777), but other soldiers' sons were not so keen on military service.

The civil and foreign wars of Constantine made heavy demands on Roman manpower. In AD 319, the emperor complained that the sons of some veterans were refusing to perform compulsory military service, while others made themselves incapable of serving by cutting off fingers. The emperor punished such 'cowards' by forcing them to act as decurions (*Theodosian Code* 7.22.1). Not to be confused with the cavalry officer, the civilian *decurio* was a member of a town council responsible for local administration, public works and tax collection. The position was hereditary, and the duties were so onerous and costly that some preferred to join the army! In AD 326, Constantine grumbled about decurions and other public servants evading their responsibilities by 'running away to the legions' (ibid. 12.1.13).

In the legions of Diocletian and Constantine, the sons of veterans rubbed shoulders with former farm hands and herders, members of the cultivated but impoverished municipal elite, and even the sons of Roman knights. Valerius Anatolius was the son of Petronius Castor, an *eques Romanus*, but the privileges of the father's membership of the ancient equestrian order did not extend to the son. Anatolius was just a *miles* of *legio II Herculia* (*CIL* VI 37102).

Scene from the Arch of Galerius at Thessalonica (AD 303). The emperor harangues his guardsmen and legionaries from a tribunal. Note the *vexillum* banners of legionary detachments and the *dracones* (dragons), which were replacing the old-style hand-topped centurial standards. Galerius may have started his military career in *legio V Macedonica*. (© G. Churchard)

Length of service

In the 1st century AD, service in the legions was fixed at 25 years, but it became common to hold discharge ceremonies every second year, and so half of all legionaries served for 26 years (e.g. *ILS* 2303, listing legionaries of *III Augusta* recruited in AD 140–141 and discharged in 166). By the end of the 2nd century AD, service was still a notional 25 years, but it seems that all legionaries were retained for 26 years before *honesta missio* (honourable discharge) and veteran privileges were granted. In AD 213, the emperor Caracalla ruled that veteran privileges would be granted to legionaries of excellent reputation who had been invalided out of the army, so long as they had completed at least 20 years of service (*Justinianic Code* 5.65.1, but note *CIL* VI 3373, which records a legionary invalided out of *II Parthica* after 19 years on medical grounds, but who was still granted an honourable discharge).

During the Persian War of AD 242–244, the bulk of *legio II Parthica* was campaigning in Mesopotamia. A skeleton crew, under the command of a *primus pilus*, was left in the legion's base at Albanum, near Rome. This unit (*reliquatio*) included men recruited in AD 216 and 218. In AD 242 and 244 respectively, these men were honourably discharged and commemorated their completion of service by setting up dedications in Rome and Albanum for the safe return of the emperors Gordian II and Philip from the East (*AE* 1981, 134; *ILS* 505). One of the new recruits drafted in to replace these men was Aurelius Iustinus. He died, while still in service, with 33 *stipendia*, during the reign of Aurelian (AD 270–275) (*AE* 1975, 171).

From the reign of Diocletian, a legionary could hope for honourable discharge after only 20 years of service (*Justinianic Code* 7.64.9). Aurelius Domitianus, a *beneficiarius* (clerk) in a detachment of *legio I Adiutrix* at Aquileia, was discharged after 20 years' service. He was only 40 when he died, and must have expired shortly after becoming a veteran (*CIL* V 894). Domitianus' epitaph states that he was 'accepted for discharge'. Although retirement could be applied for after 20 years of service, it was not granted automatically. Moreover, legionaries who did, or were compelled on medical grounds to, retire after 20 years, received lesser privileges than those who served longer. This is made clear by an edict of AD 311. A legionary who had served for 20 years would receive exemption from the poll tax for himself and his wife, but a legionary who had 'completed the *stipendia legitima*', was granted five exemptions; the three extra exemptions could presumably be extended to other members of his family (*AE* 1937, 232).

MOUNTED LEGIONARY *LANCIARIUS*, AD 284

By the close of the 3rd century AD, the legions had substantial complements of *lanciarii*, specialist fighters who fought with the light *lancia* javelin. Some *lanciarii* were mounted, providing the legion, or legionary *vexillatio* (detachment), with a highly useful corps of light cavalry in addition to the *equites* (regular legionary cavalry) and *promoti* ('promoted' cavalry).

In this reconstruction, the javelins of the *lanciarius* are carried in a case attached to the horse's saddle (**1**) (cf. Josephus, *Jewish War* 3.96). The *lanciarius* wears light armour of padded fabric (**2**), similar to a medieval aketon, known as a *thoracomachus* (*De Rebus Bellicis* 15). His helmet is of the new 'ridge' type with a two-part skull and attached neck and cheek guards. Other multi-part iron helmets were coming into service at this time (**3**), but older helmets with the bowl and neck guard made in one piece, like the bronze example from Buch (**4**), would still have been in use. The *lanciarius* is armed with two swords: a longer cut-and-thrust weapon (see **5** for the blade), and a short sword known as a *semispathium* ('half sword', Vegetius 2.15). The traditional dagger (*pugio*), with its waisted blade, was going out of use; a long, single-edged knife carried in a bronze scabbard might have been used in its place (**6**).

The edict does not reveal how many years constituted the *stipendia legitima*, 'the legitimate length of service', but it was probably still 25 or 26 years. Valerius Genialis, standard-bearer of a detachment of *legio II Italica*, had completed 26 *stipendia* when he died in AD 312 (*ILS* 2346). In AD 325, Constantine set the *stipendia legitima* at 24 years. Discharge after 20 years was still possible but, as before, with fewer veterans' benefits (*Theodosian Code* 7.20.4). Officers tended to serve far longer than ordinary soldiers. Flavius Abinnaeus, commander of an auxiliary unit in Egypt, entered military service in AD 304/5 and retired *c.* 351 (Bell 1962).

Pay

When he seized power in AD 235, the emperor Maximinus doubled military pay. Maximinus had risen through the ranks, beginning his military career as a horseman in an auxiliary cavalry unit. In an age of high inflation, he knew a massive increase in pay would cement the loyalty of the army to his new regime. Maximinus' legionary pay rates were 1,800 silver *denarii* for a legionary infantryman and 2,100 for a legionary *eques* (horseman). *Equites* received more pay to cover the costs of fodder and equine equipment. Under-officers (*principales*) received higher rates of pay. *Sesquiplicarii*, such as the *tesserarius*, earned 50 per cent above the basic rate. Senior *principales*, like the *optio* and *signifer* (standard-bearer), were *duplicarii*, that is men on double pay. As noted above, a legionary who had performed brave deeds was decorated with a torque and received the honorific title *torquatus*. Such men were made *duplarii* or *duplares*, doubling their pay grade and perhaps also ration allowance (*ILS* 2434; Vegetius 2.7). This was spare change compared to the pay of centurions. The centurions of cohorts II to X earned 15 times the basic legionary rate. The *primi ordines*, the centurions of the first cohort received 30 times the basic rate, while the *primus pilus* was paid a staggering 108,000 *denarii*, 60 times the basic rate (M. A. Speidel 1992).

Inflation soared throughout the 3rd century AD, but military pay did not increase accordingly. In AD 300, the basic annual *stipendium* of the legionary was still 1,800 *denarii* (the *denarius* was by then a unit of value rather than an actual coin). This was paid in three instalments, usually in arrears. This basic amount was supplemented by *annona* (rations or a cash allowance), *salgamum* (rations of oil and salt) and *donativum*. The latter was a 'gift' of cash or bullion paid on the anniversaries of imperial accessions, birthdays and when a pair of emperors

Porphyry statue of the Tetrarchs – Diocletian, Maximian and their Caesars, Galerius and Constantius – at Venice. The basic military *stipendium* was supplemented with special donatives paid on the accession days, birthdays and consulships of the four emperors. (© A. Haye)

assumed the consulship. On the accession day, birthday or consulate of an Augustus, a legionary would receive 2,500 *denarii*, and 1,200 *denarii* on the anniversary or consulate of a Caesar (Duncan-Jones 1990 on *P. Beatty Panop.* 2; *contra* Jones 1964, 1,257–1,259, which suggests the rates as 1,250 and 625 *denarii*).

Jones suggested that legionaries received eight donatives per year, one for each accession day and birthday of an emperor. Using his figures, this would amount to 7,500 *denarii*, and an extra 1,250 to 2,500 would be gifted if a pair of emperors assumed the consulship. Duncan-Jones suggests that there were only four donatives per year, that is one per accession day and birthday of the Augustus and Caesar ruling in the half of the Empire in which a legionary was serving. Even so, on Duncan-Jones' higher rates, a legionary would receive at least 10,000 *denarii*, five-and-a-half times his *stipendium*.

While under-officers and higher ranks received *annona* and other ration allowances commensurate with their *stipendium*, it is interesting to note that the rates for the regular donatives appear to have been the same for all ranks of legionaries.

On 1 January AD 300, Leontius, *praepositus* (commander) of a detachment of *promoti* cavalry of *legio II Traiana* at Tentyra in Egypt, received 18,000 *denarii*, the first instalment of his *stipendium*. The wage and the probable size of his detachment (77 troopers) allows us to identify Leontius as a centurion of, or equivalent to, *primi ordini* rank. He earned 30 times the pay of a legionary footman. On 20 November AD 299, the accession day of Diocletian,

Officers and *principales* of *legio II Flavia Constantia* (named in honour of Constantius I) depicted on a wall painting in the legionary fortress, which incorporated the ancient Egyptian temple at Luxor, *c.* AD 300. The substantial pay and donatives received by these men is reflected in expensively embroidered tunics and their *sagum* cloaks. (© Walwyn)

Leontius received 2,500 *denarii*, and the same amount was gifted to him on the emperor's birthday on 22 December (*P.Beatty Panop.* 2.196–207). This was still the standard donative during the reign of Constantine.

Another pay receipt from Egypt shows that an unnamed *praepositus* received 36,000 *denarii* on 1 September, the third instalment of his *stipendium*. The amount identifies him as being a senior centurion equivalent in rank to the old *primus pilus*. Five weeks earlier, on 25 July, the *praepositus* had received a donative of 2,500 *denarii*. That day was the anniversary of Constantine's accession, and so dates the pay slip to after AD 324, when Egypt came under his control (*P.Oxy.* 7.1047).

Extraordinary donatives were more valuable. The donatives paid to *protectores*, like Florius Baudio, and higher officers who had participated in victorious campaigns, or on special imperial anniversaries (marking an emperor's fifth, tenth or 20th year of rule, etc.) were very large. For example, in AD 297, the *protector* Vitalianus (who would later fight in Constantine's Italian campaign with Baudio) received gold coins and medallions to the value of 59 *aurei* (Tomlin 2006). This was his reward for serving in Constantius I's reconquest of Britain from Allectus. In Diocletian's monetary reform of AD 301, a gold *aureus* was worth 1,200 *denarii*: Vitalianus' victory donative was therefore equivalent to 70,800 *denarii*. In AD 303, on the *vicennalia* (20th anniversary) of Diocletian's assumption of power, Vitalianus received 138 *aurei*. The amount, more than double what he received in AD 297, probably reflects a promotion in rank.

The legionaries of Diocletian and Constantine, even those receiving the basic *stipendium* and supplements, were relatively well off. In the preamble to his *Edict on Maximum Prices* (AD 301), Diocletian claimed that criminal profiteers had forced prices so high that a single purchase could wipe out a soldier's donatives and *stipendium*. The emperor exaggerated somewhat.

A *librarius* (clerk) of *legio II Herculia* could afford a fine sarcophagus (*AE* 1952, 231: the inscription warns that anyone caught tampering with it will be fined 20,000 *denarii*). On a memorial set up for his wife, the former *optio* Aurelius Gaius noted how it had been paid for from 'the profits of my labours' (*AE* 1981, 777). Like Gaius, Aurelius Flavinus was an *optio*, and therefore a senior *principalis* in receipt of double pay. This allowed him to amass a considerable sum in his century's bank, which was administered by the standard bearer (cf. Vegetius 2.20). Flavinus' exceptional tombstone, depicting him with his long staff of office, horse and *calo* (servant), cost 10,000 *denarii*, almost three years' *stipendium* (*CIL* V 895; Franzoni 1987, nr. 15). When he drafted his will in AD 320, the wealth of Valerius Aion, a centurion of the *equites promoti* of *legio II Traiana*, was substantial: silver talents to the value of 299,950 *denarii*, eight gold coins (the value of which is uncertain due to the fluctuating price of gold since AD 301, but certainly a five-figure sum in *denarii*), as well as other goods and property (*P.Col.* 7.188).

Prospects and promotion

How long did it take a legionary to achieve specialist status or promotion to a higher pay grade?

The epitaph of Aurelius Iustinus informs us that he was a *munifex*, a soldier who had to perform basic and menial duties (*munera*), for seven years. Aged 24, he became an *eques* (trooper), and remained in that post until his death four years later (*ILS* 2332). It would appear that the *equites*, on account of their specialist tactical function, were *immunes*, that is immune from fatigues.

Valerius Longinianus was *optio* for 15 years and centurion for another six, but his epitaph fails to mention his service before promotion to *principalis* (*ILS* 2670). Aurelius Flavinus, the possible Aquileian recruit, became an *optio* after 14 years. He remained in that rank for a decade, with death taking him before he could advance to the rank of centurion (*CIL* V 895).

Valerius Aulucentius did achieve the rank of centurion, but his epitaph emphasizes that he spent 14 years as *miles gregarius*, a common soldier (*CIL* V 940). He presumably progressed through the tactical grades in the century: *tesserarius* (officer of the watchword), *optio*, and perhaps also *signifer*. Like Flavinus, Aulucentius is portrayed on his impressive tombstone with a staff of office (*vitis*), horse and *calo* (Franzoni 1987, nr. 20). The carving on Flavinus' memorial is fine and naturalistic, but that of Aulucentius' tombstone is influenced by the powerful abstract style of the official portraiture of the Tetrarchs.

Should we assume that Flavinus and Aulucentius led legionary cavalry? Not necessarily. Neither man is described as an *eques* (cavalryman) or belonging to a unit of *equites* or *equites promoti* (see below). Contrast their comrade at Aquileia, the centurion Iulius, who is identified as *magister equitum*, 'master of cavalry' (*ILS* 2333). If Flavinus and Aulucentius were cavalrymen we would expect them to be described as such. The Romans were sensitive about matters of rank, seniority and precedence. Recall how the epitaph of Aurelius Iustinus stressed his promotion from infantry *munifex* to cavalry *eques*. Valerius Quintus, another legionary of *XI Claudia* at Aquileia, died while still training to become an *eques*. His epitaph announces that he was *discens equitum*, a trainee cavalryman, thus marking him as a cut above the *munifices* (*CIL* V 944).

Valerius Aulucentius, a Thracian centurion of *legio XI Claudia*, with his horse and *calo* (servant) (*CIL* V 940). Aulucentius' rank is indicated by his *vitis*, a short, tapering staff. (© J. Vermeersch)

It is probable that the horse was granted as a privilege of rank to all senior *principales* and centurions (cf. the gravestone of Flavius Augustalis, a Constantinian centurion at Aquileia: Franzoni 1987, nr. 21). The horse was certainly a valuable status symbol. In his price edict of AD 301, Diocletian set the cost of a best quality war horse at 36,000 *denarii* (Crawford & Reynolds 1979, 177). Flavinus and Aulucentius may have ridden when the army was on the march, but in battle they would have fought on foot. As the principal tactical subunit of the legion, the *centuria* (century) required a commander (centurion) and under-officers (like the *optio* and *signifer*) who fought in the front rank and led by example (Cowan 2013, 27–30).

The career of Aurelius Gaius

The most detailed career of the age belongs to Aurelius Gaius. It is recorded on a funerary monument set up for his wife, but the bulk of the inscription actually concerns Gaius' tenure in the legions. The decoration even depicts Gaius with his *calones*, war horses and weapons (Drew-Bear 1981; *AE* 1981, 777).

Aurelius Gaius was born in Pessinus (Ballihisar) in Phrygia, but he joined a European legion, *I Italica*, based at Novae (Svishtov) on the Danubian frontier in Moesia. He was subsequently selected for transfer to the German legion *VIII Augusta*, and later served in *I Iovia* in Scythia (the far east of Moesia, by the Black Sea). The final legion was created by Diocletian in the later AD 280s.

The inscription goes on to lists Gaius' ranks: *tiro* (recruit), trainee cavalryman, cavalry *lanciarius*, and a succession of posts as *optio*. Gaius presumably progressed from trainee horseman to specialist mounted *lanciarius* in *legio I Italica*. From *lanciarius* (specialist fighter with the *lancia* javelin) he made the leap to *optio*, and was successively *optio* to a *centurio triarius*, a *centurio ordinatus* and a *centurio princeps*. The *centurio triarius* was a 'centurion of the third rank'. The *centurio ordinatus* is probably identical with the *centurio ordinarius*, a senior centurion of the first cohort. The *centurio princeps* was perhaps the chief centurion of the legion (below). Finally, while serving in *legio I Iovia*, he was an *optio* attached to the *comitatus*, the retinue of one of the emperors.

Gaius then informs us that 'he travelled around the empire'. This is an understatement. Despite being fragmentary, the list of provinces and regions, as well as areas beyond the frontiers, he visited is astonishing. It includes Asia, Caria, Lydia, Lycaonia, Cilicia, Syria Phoenice, Arabia, Palestine, Egypt, Alexandria, India, Mesopotamia, Cappadocia, Galatia, Bythinia (all in the Near East), and then Thrace and Moesia in Europe. Gaius proceeds to note that he had been to the trans-Danubian lands of the Carpi (at least once), to Sarmatia four times, to Viminacium in Pannonia, and to the lands of the Goths on two occasions. The list is completed by Germany, Dardania, Dalmatia, Pannonia, Gaul, Spain and Mauretania. 'After all these tribulations' Gaius returned to Phrygia and settled in the village of Cotiaeum, in the territory of Pessinus.

It is possible to make sense of Gaius' travels if we assume he was recruited into *legio I Italica* at the time of the Persian War of Carus and Numerian, either to bring the legion up to strength for the campaign, or to replenish the casualties it sustained in the fighting (AD 283/4). If the mention of Viminacium (Kostolac) refers to the battle of the River Margus (Morava) where, in the late spring of AD 285, Diocletian narrowly defeated Carinus (Diocletian was camped at Viminacium, just to the east of the river, and Carinus to the west of it at Mons Aureus

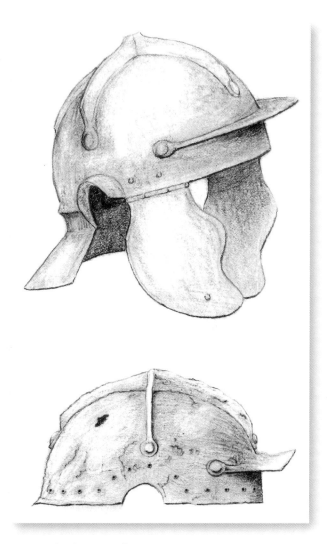

Old military equipment was stockpiled and employed when necessary (cf. Zosimus 3.3), as demonstrated by this 2nd century AD helmet, which was savagely modified to conform to the fashion of the 4th century AD. (© Steven D. P. Richardson)

(Smederevo): Eutropius 9.20), we can attempt to untangle the rest of Gaius' rambling geographical list.

After his victory over Carinus, Diocletian proceeded to Italy and perhaps visited Rome. By autumn AD 285, he had returned north, crossed the Danube and was campaigning against the Sarmatians. This would be the first of Gaius' four expeditions into Sarmatia. Gaius' detachment (he was presumably still with *I Italica*) then accompanied the emperor to the eastern provinces. In Syria, Diocletian was involved in negotiations with Persian ambassadors and the establishment of new frontier fortifications (AD 287). Diocletian then returned to Europe, and from the province of Raetia, invaded free Germany and defeated the Alamanni and Iuthungi (AD 288). This campaign may account for the mention of Germany in Gaius' list.

Despite their defeat in AD 285, the Sarmatians were not broken and were threatening New Dacia. Diocletian campaigned against them again in summer AD 289 (hence Gaius' second Sarmatian expedition). He won a major victory and assumed the title *Sarmaticus Maximus*, 'conqueror of the Sarmatians'. In the following year, Diocletian was back in the East, this time fighting the Saraceni Arabs (hence Gaius' visit to 'Arabia').

Gaius' two forays into the lands of the Goths may date to AD 292/3, when Diocletian assumed the title *Gothicus Maximus* (*AE* 1936, 10). Diocletian established the Tetrarchy in AD 293, and Gaius found himself in the field army of the new Caesar, Galerius. It was with Galerius that Gaius travelled to Egypt, visiting Alexandria and 'India', meaning the south of Egypt, where he was involved in the suppression of a revolt in the Thebaid (AD 293–294). The seriousness of the fighting is indicated by the victory titles assumed by Galerius – *Aegyptiacus* and *Thebaicus Maximus*, and the skills of a battle-hardened *lanciarius* like Gaius would have been invaluable. Gaius was probably still serving in *I Italica*. Galerius' army included detachments from the three other Moesian legions: *IV Flavia*, *VII Claudia* and *XI Claudia* (*P. Oxy* 1.43 recto).

After settling Egypt, Galerius was involved in preparations for war against Persia, but Gaius returned to Europe. Diocletian was responsible for the 'annihilation of the Carpi' in AD 296 (*Latin Panegyrics* 8(5).5.2), but it is unlikely that this was the occasion of Gaius' sojourn in the land of the Carpi. Diocletian and Galerius would wage other campaigns against the Carpi (see page XX); AD 296 was probably the year of Gaius' transfer to *legio VIII Augusta* at Argentorate (Strasbourg) in Germany.

While the Caesar Constantius and his praetorian prefect, Asclepiodotus, reconquered Britain in AD 296, the Augustus Maximian took up station on the Rhine frontier and shielded Gaul from German raids. Maximian then marched through Gaul to Spain where he fought an unspecified enemy (*P. Argent.* 480, 1, verso 3), perhaps raiders from North Africa. By the spring of AD 297, he was in Mauretania and conducting a war against the Quinquegentiani, a tribal confederation. Victory was achieved the following year and in AD 299 Maximian sailed for Italy and celebrated his triumph in Rome.

The geographical sequence of Gaul, Spain and Mauretania in Gaius' list mirrors the movements of Maximian in AD 296–298. Gaius, having been transferred to *VIII Augusta* (presumably to take up the post of *optio* to a senior centurion), was almost certainly a member of Maximian's field army.

As we have seen, the detachment of *legio XI Claudia* at Aquileia supplied a contingent to Maximian's army; the Thracian legionary Aurelius Dizo was killed in Africa (*CIL* V 893). The army also contained detachments from Raetia's *III Italica*, Noricum's *II Italica* and Scythia's *II Herculia*. *Legio III Italica* was represented by cohorts I and II, and *II Herculia* by cohorts VII and X (*AE* 1972, 710; *ILS* 4195). Only one cohort *of legio II Italica* (*cohors VIII*) is attested, but the presence of another is likely (*AE* 1972, 709). Maximian may also have taken a detachment of the German legion *I Minervia*; the gravestone of its *aquilifer* (eagle-bearer), Aurelius Iovinus, at Theveste (Tébessa) suggests a detachment that included the legion's first cohort (*AE* 1995, 1710).

BELIEF AND BELONGING

Christians in a pagan army

Aurelius Gaius was a Christian. His inscription concludes with the statement that he set up the monument in honour of his 'dearest wife, as a memorial until the resurrection'. This has led to the assumption that Gaius was forced out of the army soon after AD 299. Diocletian, a conservative pagan, was suspicious of Christians and in AD 303 launched a brutal persecution. Prior to this, in AD 299, Diocletian and Galerius believed that Christian members of the imperial retinue had jinxed a pagan divination ceremony. Diocletian was incensed and ordered that all soldiers were to sacrifice to the gods who ensured the strength and prosperity of the Empire. Those soldiers who refused to sacrifice would be revealed as Christians and dismissed from the army (Lactantius, *On the Deaths of the Persecutors* 10.1–5). However, not all Christian soldiers chose to disobey the order to sacrifice (cf. Eusebius, *History of the Church* 8.4.3). Gaius was probably such a pragmatist. Until Christianity was officially tolerated in AD 311–313, it is likely that Gaius kept his faith to himself, and that his service in *legio I Iovia* and the imperial retinue dates to the first decade of the 4th century AD.

It is possible that Gaius, recruited in *c*. AD 283/4, applied for honourable discharge in AD 303/4, during the Great Persecution. His third and fourth visits to Sarmatia, and his time in the land of the Carpi, could have occurred during the campaigns of Galerius in AD 301–303. If Gaius completed the *stipendia legitima* of 25–26 years, he may also have participated in Diocletian's final campaign (against the Carpi in AD 304)

Galerius believed he was sired by Mars, the god of war, and was an enthusiastic persecutor of the Christians. However, while dying of cancer in AD 311, he issued an edict of toleration. (© G. Churchard)

and accompanied Galerius on his last expeditions against the Sarmatians and Carpi (AD 306/7 and 308/9). As a member of the *comitatus*, Gaius might have witnessed Diocletian's abdication at Nicomedia in AD 305 (Lactantius, *On the Deaths of the Persecutors* 19).

Gaius did not achieve promotion to the rank of centurion, but compared to the average *miles gregarius* who achieved no greater status than *immunis*, he had enjoyed a varied career, rising from a lowly recruit to a senior under-officer of the imperial retinue. He had marched, rode and sailed thousands of miles across the Empire and campaigned far beyond its frontiers. He had fought other legionaries (at the Margus), rebels and a host of barbarians. When he finally retired from the army, he probably did so as a wealthy man. As an *optio*, he would have received double pay and increased rations, especially when he served in the *comitatus* (cf. Rea 1985: a quadruple ration allowance was given to a junior member of Galerius' *comitatus* in Egypt). As well as 20 to 26 years' worth of the regular donatives, his continuous service in the field armies of Diocletian, Maximian and Galerius meant he would have been the recipient of many victory donatives and would have had ample opportunities to take plunder from the enemy. (For other interpretations of

Gaius' career and movements, see Drew-Bear 1981; Barnes 1996, 542–543; Colombo 2010.)

It is suggested here that Aurelius Gaius reconciled his faith with military service. Other Christian legionaries could not. On 21 July, AD 298, Marcellus, *hastatus* of the first cohort, threw down his *vitis*, military belt (*balteus*) and sword and declared he could not renew his military oath (*sacramentum*, 'sacred bond') because he was a Christian. Marcellus did so before the standards of his legion, probably on the parade ground, because 21 July was an imperial anniversary, possibly the accession day or birthday of Maximian (Barnes 1996, 538–539). He was detained and tried some months later. He continued to espouse his Christianity, stating it was not proper for a Christian to engage in military service, but this was the year preceding Diocletian's purge of Christians from the army and Agricolanus, the deputy praetorian prefect conducting the trial, had little interest in the soldier's faith. Marcellus was found guilty because he had broken his military oath and defiled the office of centurion. He was decapitated with a sword, a method of execution reserved for persons of rank (*Passion of St. Marcellus* (Lanata)).

Fifteen versions of the *Passion of St. Marcellus* are known. Only one of these identifies Marcellus' unit (named as the Egyptian legion, *II Traiana*) and its evidence is suspect. But the majority of versions agree that Marcellus was tried and executed in Tingis (Tangier) in Mauretania Tingitana. He was, therefore, a senior centurion in one of the legionary vexillations in the field army Maximian raised to fight in the African war of AD 297–298. He might even have been an associate of Aurelius Gaius.

Pagan legionaries

The edicts tolerating Christianity issued by Galerius in AD 311, and by Constantine and Licinius, and even Maximinus Daia, in AD 313, probably meant little to the majority of legionaries. Most soldiers of this era were pagans, and remained so until late in the reign of Constantine (below). Clear evidence comes from funerary inscriptions. For example, when they died aged eight and one, Valerius Castus, *centurio ordinarius* of *legio I Iovia*,

LEFT

Aquiliferi (eagle-bearers) on the Arch of Constantine, Rome (AD 315). The *aquila* was the chief standard of the legion. The *genius* (divine spirit) of the unit was thought to reside in the *aquila*. (© RHC Archive)

RIGHT

Hercules (left) and lion (right, only the hind quarters survive) shield blazons from the Arch of Galerius. The demigod Hercules was the particular *conservator* of Maximian and was invoked as a protector of all the emperors. The lion appears as the legionary emblem on a shield from Dura-Europos (*c.* AD 256). (© T. Efthimiadis)

commended his infant daughters to the *di manes*, the spirits of the Underworld (*AE* 1989, 641).

Religious dedications demonstrate how the traditional Roman gods, as well as Oriental and Celtic deities, and the *genii* (divine spirits of places and organisations) continued to be revered.

In AD 283, Aurelius Decimus was governor of Numidia and he made a dedication to the *genius* (spirit) of the fortress of *legio III Augusta* (*ILS* 2291). Decimus had been a senior legionary officer. Prior to his governorship, he was *princeps peregrinorum*, the commander of the *frumentarii* based at the Castra Peregrina (Fort of the Foreigners) in Rome. The *frumentarii* were legionaries who acted as couriers between the provincial capitals and Rome, but the emperors also found them useful as spies and assassins. They were so feared and unpopular that Diocletian disbanded their unit (Aurelius Victor 39.44).

Between AD 286 and 293, a prefect of *legio IIII Flavia* honoured the *genius* of his legion, perhaps on the occasion of his retirement or promotion to a higher post (*ILS* 2292). Aurelius Maximus, a centurion of *II Adiutrix*, erected an altar to Jupiter Best and Greatest and the '*genius* of this place' in fulfilment of a vow made during the reign of Diocletian (*CIL* III 10060). The place was Metulum (Munjava) in Dalmatia. The nature of Maximus' vow can only be guessed at, but he clearly felt the *genius* of Metulum to be a reality and of some importance.

Jupiter, chief of the gods in the Roman pantheon, was frequently invoked for the health and safety of the emperors (e.g. *AE* 2009, 1116, by a prefect of *II Adiutrix*). The god was the particular *conservator*, protective deity,

Cylindrical legionary *scutum* from Dura-Europos (*c.* AD 256), decorated with winged Victories, an eagle and lion. Similar devices occur on shields on the Arches of Galerius and Constantine (AD 303, 315). (© K. Steel)

Coin of Constantine celebrating the 'glory of the army'. The standard between the two soldiers is a *labarum*, the Christian battle standard. (© RHC Archive)

of Diocletian (*ILS* 631). Maximian's protective deity was Hercules (*ILS* 632). In AD 287 Aurelius Firminus, prefect of *II Adiutrix*, dedicated an altar to 'Hercules of the Emperors' in fulfilment of a vow. Firminus describes himself as 'prefect … formerly *protector*', and the vow to Hercules may have concerned his desire to be promoted from the protectorate to command of a legion.

Mars, the god of war, was the *conservator* of Galerius. In fact, the emperor believed he was the son of the god (*ILS* 633; Lactantius, *On the Deaths of the Persecutors* 9.9). Mars was, of course, venerated by soldiers and in AD 295 the prefect of *legio I Minervia* undertook the restoration of the shrine of Mars Militaris at Bonna (Bonn) because it had 'collapsed through old age' (*CIL* XIII 8019).

As junior emperor, Constantius I came under the special protection of Sol Invictus, the Unconquered Sun. The emperor Licinius was another devotee of Sol and commanded the soldiery to honour statues of the god (*ILS* 8940, AD 317/24). It was to the Sun that Licinius' legionaries prayed for victory before the battle on the plain of Ergenus in AD 313 (see commentary to Plate E).

Closely associated with Sol was Mithras, a curious bull-slaying divinity imported from Persia. Worshippers of Mithras may have believed in some form of resurrection or afterlife. In AD 298, having survived Maximian's African War, legionaries of *II Herculia* dedicated a promised monument to the 'Invincible God Mithras' (*ILS* 4195).

Gradual conversion

Following his conversion to Christianity in AD 312, Constantine was outwardly tolerant of pagans but he banned animal sacrifice, removing the key act of pagan ceremony and means of interaction with the gods. Constantine seems to have identified the Christian God with Sol, his original pagan protector, and it was on the *dies Solis* (Sunday) that his Christian soldiers were given time off to worship. The emperor also conceived of a special 'church parade' for his pagan soldiers:

> With regard to those who were as yet ignorant of divine truth, he provided by a second statute that they should appear on each Lord's day on an open plain near the city, and there, at a given signal, offer to God with one accord a prayer which they had previously learnt. He admonished them that their

 B

TRAINING: OPEN AND CLOSE BATTLE ORDER

Here we see two legionary *centuriae* (centuries) in a mock battle. One century advances in open order, in four staggered ranks of 20. This had long been the favoured formation of the subunits of the legion, allowing the individual *milites* (soldiers) room to throw their javelins and then fight with swords (cf. Polybius 18.30.6–10). The other *centuria* advances in a close order of eight ranks and ten files. The formation was, like a phalanx, more often used defensively against cavalry than offensively (e.g. Arrian, *Ectaxis contra Alanos* 15–18). At the centre of the front rank of each *centuria* is a *signifer* (standard-bearer) with a gold *draco* (dragon) standard with a long red fabric tail. The *signum* (standard) showed the legionaries where to advance and acted as a rallying point. The *signifer* (later known as the *draconarius*) stands to the left of the *centurio* (centurion), commander of the *centuria*, who is distinguished by a gilded helmet with a red plume. The centurion's helmet also acted as a *signum*; where he led, the legionaries followed (Vegetius 2.13, 16).

confidence should not rest in their spears, or armor, or bodily strength, but that they should acknowledge the supreme God as the giver of every good, and of victory itself; to whom they were bound to offer their prayers with due regularity, uplifting their hands toward heaven, and raising their mental vision higher still to the king of heaven, on whom they should call as the Author of victory, their Preserver, Guardian, and Helper. The emperor himself prescribed the prayer to be used by all his troops, commanding them, to pronounce the following words in the Latin tongue:

'We acknowledge thee the only God: we own thee, as our King and implore thy succor. By thy favor have we gotten the victory: through thee are we mightier than our enemies. We render thanks for thy past benefits, and trust thee for future blessings. Together we pray to thee, and beseech thee long to preserve to us, safe and triumphant, our emperor Constantine and his pious sons.' Such was the duty to be performed on Sunday by his troops, and such the prayer they were instructed to offer up to God. (Eusebius, *Life of Constantine* 4.19.1–20.1)

Pagan soldiers would have initially identified the unnamed 'only god' in this monotheistic prayer with Sol Invictus; Christ was presumably conflated with, and then gradually supplanted, the Unconquered Sun. At the time of Constantine's death in AD 337, the conversion of the army was not complete, but the process was irreversible. The principal battle standard of the army was now the Christian *Labarum* (Eusebius, *Life of Constantine* 1.31); all soldiers bore some kind of Christian insignia (cross or *Chi-Rho* monogram) on their shields (ibid. 4.21); and their *sacramentum*, sacred military oath, was sworn to 'God, Christ, the Holy Spirit, and the Majesty of the Emperor' (Vegetius 2.5).

TRAINING

Constantine wearing a very simplified ridge-type helmet. The emperor was a consummate warrior and exemplar of traditional Roman *virtus*. (© RHC Archive)

We are not well informed about training and training instructors. It is likely that the ranks of legionary training officer attested in the 2nd and 3rd centuries AD continued into our period, and that an important new instructor, *campidoctor*, was introduced into the legions.

Campidoctores and warrior ethos

The *armatura* was a junior but important instructor, taking his title from the weapons drill of the same name. Those trained in the *armatura*, a drill involving javelins, the sword and shield, could outfight anyone (Vegetius 1.13). Mastery of the *armatura* was essential for promotion to the rank of centurion and the drill was practised daily by all soldiers, including the emperor (Vegetius 2.14, 23; Ammianus Marcellinus 21.16.7 on the expertise of Constantius II in the infantry *armatura*). It is uncertain how many *armatura* instructors were in a legion, but in the period AD 211–222, *legio II Adiutrix* had enough to form a *collegium*, or association (ILS 2363).

Vegetius was writing at the end of the 4th century AD. In his day, the *armatura* was the preserve of *campidoctores*. These 'field instructors' were senior centurions and ranked third in the command structure of the Late Roman legion (Rance 2007). The rank of *armidoctor*, a senior weapons instructor, existed in *legio XV Apollinaris* during the Flavian era (AD 69–96). *Campidoctores* first appear in provincial and imperial guards units from the end of the 2nd century AD. The presence of *campidoctores* in the early imperial legions has been assumed (Cowan 2013, 16–18), but they are not clearly attested in a legionary context until the mid-4th century AD. It may have been Constantine who introduced the rank of *campidoctor* into the legions, or retitled those centurions concerned with training, when he started to reform the army in AD 325 (Aurelius Victor 41.13).

Ammianus Marcellinus paints a fascinating picture of the legionary *campidoctores* involved in the defence of Amida (Diyarbakir) in AD 359. They preferred not to guard the ramparts, but to make sallies and fight the besieging Sassanid Persians on open ground. The gates of the city were eventually barred to prevent their risky sorties, but the legionaries threatened to kill senior officers and were permitted to make one final attack at night.

Armed with swords and axes, they killed the Persian guards, entered the enemy camp and advanced on the tent of the king, Shapur II. They never reached it. Ammianus, a staff officer and an eyewitness to the battle, describes how the legionaries cut down countless Persians, including noble commanders, but they were eventually forced to retreat by the volume of the arrows loosed by the Persian archers. Courage carried the legionaries only so far, and cohesive discipline was re-asserted during the retreat. Ammianus describes with admiration how the legionaries made their orderly fighting retreat 'as if to music'.

Four hundred legionaries were killed in the night-long battle, but the Persians suffered such heavy casualties that they sought a three-day truce. On the order of Constantius II, the *campidoctores* who led the attack were commemorated at Edessa with statues depicting them in full armour (Ammianus Marcellinus 19.6).

Despite their responsibility for training and instilling discipline, these *campidoctores* had threatened mutiny and then lost their lives in a heroic but futile mission. This was classic Roman military behaviour. The legionaries at Amida were Gauls or Germans who served a now Christian empire, but like Pullo and Vorenus, the famously berserk centurions of Julius Caesar, their instinct was to attack, even when under siege. Like Caesar's centurions, they were motivated by the wish to maintain and enhance their reputations for *virtus*, a quality that encompassed manliness, excellence and, above all, valour. Competition between centurions for honour and glory was believed to inspire legionaries (Caesar, *Gallic War* 5.44). This suggests why the antics of the *campidoctores* at Amida were not just tolerated, but praised and commemorated.

The Roman Army is frequently described as a 'military machine', but this imposes an inappropriate modernity. The army developed out of the war bands of the aristocratic clans of Iron Age Rome. Despite growing massively in size and complexity over the centuries, the army always retained a warrior ethos. In 221 BC, the funeral eulogy of Caecilius Metellus proclaimed he had achieved the 'ten greatest and highest objects' that mark out great men. These included having been a brave general and winning victories under his own auspices, but the most important object Metellus attained was having been a warrior (*bellator*) of the first rank (Pliny, *Natural History* 7.140).

The desire to prove one's worth as a warrior remained strong in the late 3rd and 4th centuries AD. The emperor Galerius was recalled as a 'skilled and fortunate *bellator*' (*Epitome de Caesaribus* 40.15). Bonitus the Frank, one of Constantine's generals in AD 324, and before that a legionary *praepositus*, was renowned for his *fortia facta* (brave deeds) (Ammianus Marcellinus 15.5.33). Constantine was never one to shy away from combat. In AD 302 he was a senior tribune in Galerius' *comitatus* and noted for his feats against the Sarmatians:

Cavalryman armed with an axe on a relief from Galerius' palace at Romuliana (Gamzigrad). Legionary cavalry might be armed with swords, lances, axes and even maces, and would practise their weapons drills every day (Vegetius 2.23). (© A. Chen/ISAWNYU)

He seized by the hair and carried off a fierce barbarian and threw him down at the feet of the emperor. Sent by Galerius through a swamp, he entered it on his horse and made a way for the rest of the army to the Sarmatians, of whom he slew many and won the victory for Galerius. (*Origin of Constantine* 2.3)

As emperor, Constantine led from the front and was sometimes wounded in battle (*Origin of Constantine* 5.24), but his displays of *virtus* were inspirational (*Latin Panegyrics* 4(12).29.6).

The Master of Cavalry

Legionary cavalry instructors were certainly *bellatores* of the first rank. The legionary *exercitator equitum* ('exerciser of the horsemen') of the 2nd and 3rd centuries was a high-ranking centurion, who probably also acted as the commander (*praepositus*) of the legion's cavalry in the field (cf. *ILS* 2416).

Aelius Proculinus is an interesting example of the *exercitator*. He enlisted in the same auxiliary cohort as his father, *cohors I Hemesenorum*, in AD 221 and rose to become its leading centurion. The cohort was part-mounted and included horse archers, and Proculinus would have become an expert fighter on horseback with sword, javelin, lance and bow. These skills earned him transfer to *legio II Adiutrix*, where he assumed the post

MISSILE WEAPONS AND BUTT-SPIKES

Since the 4th century BC, the legionary's fighting style was defined by two weapons: the *pilum* and the *gladius*. The *pilum*, a javelin with a long iron shank for punching through shields and armour, would be thrown at close range. The legionary would then draw his *gladius* (the word simply means 'sword', not 'short sword' as is often assumed), charge into the enemy and hack and stab until victorious. The legionary of the early 4th century AD fought in the same manner (*Latin Panegyrics* 12(9).9.6, 4(12).26.2; Lactantius, *On the Deaths of the Persecutors* 47.1–2). His sword might have been somewhat longer (referred to as a *gladius* or *spatha*), but it remained a cut-and-thrust weapon. Prior to charging to close quarters, the 4th century AD legionary could use one of a vast selection of javelins to break up the ranks of the enemy – from heavy *pila* to long-shanked *spicula* with barbed heads, or small *plumbata* darts with lead weights. Butt-spikes protected the base of the shaft of the spear or javelin from rot and could be used as a secondary weapon.

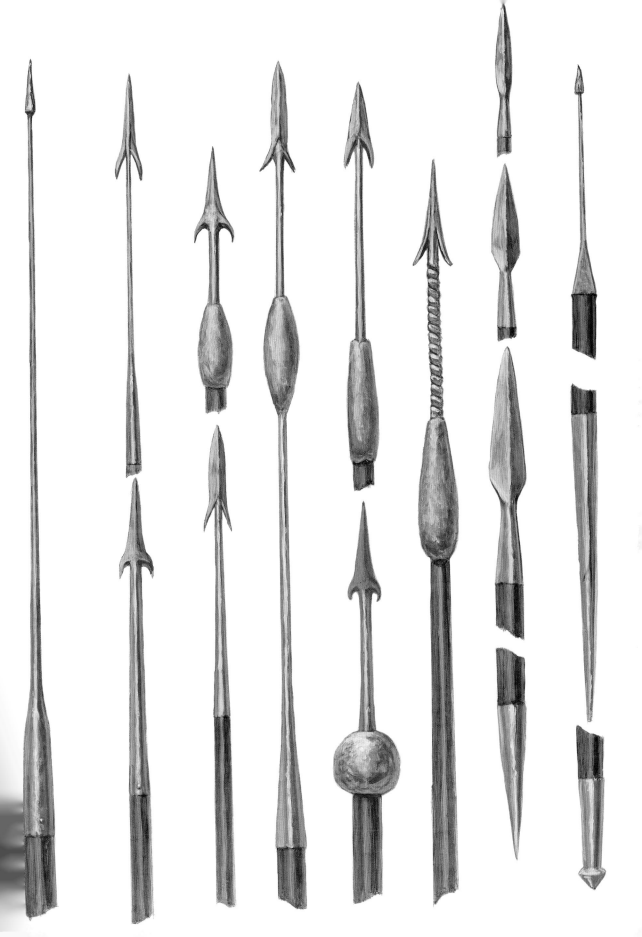

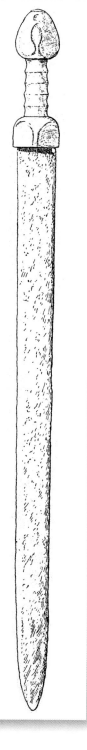

Gladius of the late 3rd century AD from Cologne. The hilt was ivory and the scabbard chape, elaborately decorated with silver and niello. (© RHC Archive)

of *centurio exercitator equitum*. Earmarked for promotion to higher rank, he was transferred to Rome and served as centurion in an urban cohort while he waited for a centurionate to become vacant in the Praetorian Guard. By AD 247 he was a centurion of the 'seventh loyal and avenging praetorian cohort', but was killed in a battle against the Carpi (*AE* 1965, 223).

The *exercitator equitum* was assisted by a *magister kampi*, the 'master of the parade ground'. During the reign of Severus Alexander (AD 222–235), the names and ranks of the members of the *schola* (club) of the horsemen of *legio III Augusta* were inscribed for posterity on a monument at Lambaesis (*CIL* VIII 2562). Geminius Extricatus is identified as *magister kampi*. The rank of Terentius Saturninus, another member of the *schola*, is abbreviated to *HAST*. It is unlikely that this is an abbreviation of *hastatus*, one of the senior centurions of legion's first cohort. Saturninus was probably a *hastiliarius* concerned with the teaching of spear (*hasta*) fighting techniques.

The training methods of Proculinus, Extricatus and Saturninus would have followed the prescriptions of the emperor Hadrian (AD 117–138), whose methods were so effective that they were still employed in the 4th century AD (Vegetius 1.27). According to Dio, Hadrian wished his soldiers 'to be drilled in every kind of battle' (69.9.3), and this meant his cavalrymen had to train in the lance and bow fighting techniques of the Parthians and Sarmatians (Arrian, *Tactica* 44). Such techniques remained essential in our era. The Sarmatians remained a major menace and Diocletian and Galerius waged many campaigns against them, while the Sassanid Persians carried on the catafract (heavily armoured cavalry) and horse archer tactics of the Parthians.

We have already encountered Iulius, the 16-year-old recruit to *legio XI Claudia*, who ended his career as a centurion at Aquileia around the year AD 300 (*ILS* 2333). After being accepted as a probationer (*probatus*), he was made *discens equitum* (trainee cavalryman). Unlike his comrade Aurelius Iustinus, who had to wait for six years (*ILS* 2332), Iulius was probably already a skilled horseman and this facilitated immediate entry into the legionary cavalry. He progressed through the grades to the post of *magister equitum*, 'master of the cavalry', who ranked as *centurio supernumerarius* (supernumerary centurion) and was the successor of the *exercitator equitum*. Iulius was, therefore, responsible for training the legionary horsemen at Aquileia, and he perhaps acted as their *praepositus*.

Legionary cavalry and infantry had to train together to ensure effective cooperation on the battlefield. In AD 128, Hadrian observed the manoeuvres of *legio III Augusta* at Lambaesis. The emperor, who had served as a legionary tribune and legate, critiqued the soldiers on their performance. His comments were written down and subsequently inscribed on a monument on the legion's parade ground. Fragments of the inscription concern the legionary *equites* charging out to engage an opponent, and then retreating into the protective ranks of the *hastati* and *principes* – see page 34 (Speidel 2006, 9–11). These exercises were still practised three times a month in the late 4th century AD (Vegetius 1.27), and one assumes that Iulius drilled his *equites* in such manoeuvres.

EQUIPMENT

The legionary infantryman was usually equipped with two long javelins called *tela*, and a medium-length cut-and-thrust sword still generally referred to as a *gladius* (*Latin Panegyrics* 12(9).9.6, 17.3; Lactantius, *On the Deaths of the Persecutors* 47.1), but sometimes known as a *spatha* (*Passion of St. Marcellus* (Lanata) 1, 3a). The sword was carried on a *balteus*, the military belt (ibid.).

Specialist fighters might be armed with multiple short *lanciae* (light javelins) or lead-weighted *mattiobarbuli* darts (Vegetius 1.17, also called *plumbatae*: 2.15). When fighting fully armoured heavy cavalry at close quarters, swords and javelins would be substituted with heavy wooden clubs or maces (Libanius, *Orations* 59.110; *Latin Panegyrics* 4(12).24.3).

Spears rarely feature in contemporary battle accounts, which are dominated by hurled *tela* and clashing *gladii*. However, Lepontius, probably a *signifer* of *legio VIII Augusta*, is depicted on his tombstone holding a heavy spear (*hasta*), while his standard (unusually a cockerel, not otherwise known as a symbol of the legion) is behind him (*CIL* XIII 5980). A standard-bearer like Lepontius, who held his standard with his left hand and had his shield slung from his shoulder, would doubtless have found the spear a useful weapon for keeping the enemy at a distance. A relief from Lentia (Linz), probably belonging to a gravestone, depicts a left-handed soldier with a spear. He was presumably a legionary of *II Italica*, which in the 4th century AD was divided between bases at Lentia and its original headquarters in neighbouring Lauriacum (Enns) (*Notitia Dignitatum, Occidentis* 34.38–39).

Legionary cavalrymen, depending on their speciality, were armed with swords, *lancia*-type javelins, maces, axes, and long *contus* lances, which had to be wielded with two hands (*P.Col.* 7.188).

Calones (servants, grooms) are sometimes depicted on the gravestones

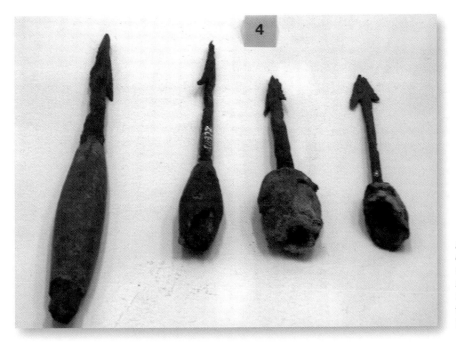

Plumbatae, lead-weighted darts, from Lauriacum, the headquarters of *legio II Italica*. According to Vegetius, a legionary would slot five of these darts behind his shield (1.17, 2.15). (© Florian Himmler)

Lepontius, standard-bearer of *legio VIII Augusta*. The bull was the usual symbol of the legion (indicating its origin as one of the legions of Julius Caesar), but Lepontius' *signum* was a cockerel. (© radiowood & RHC Archive)

of soldiers, following their deceased master with spare weapons. It is possible that they performed this role in battle, waiting behind the lines with replacement javelins and swords.

The legionary's large oval or round shield was still known as a *scutum* and his iron helmet was a *galea* (Lactantius, *On the Deaths of the Persecutors* 46.10). Body armour, of mail, scale, and perhaps even articulated plate (see commentary to Plate F), was called *lorica* and might be supplemented with armguards and greaves.

The equipment used by legionaries was not necessarily up to date. Old-fashioned, but still serviceable, fighting gear would be employed (cf. Zosimus 3.3).

LEFT
Detail of the mail shirt worn by a standard-bearer on the Great Ludovisi battle sarcophagus, *c.* AD 260. (© RHC Archive)

RIGHT
Plate from a Newstead-type *lorica segmentata* found in an early 4th century context at Carlisle, suggesting the armour was still in limited use. (© RHC Archive)

Section of an articulated limb defence from Arelape-Pöchlarn. (© Florian Himmler)

ORGANIZATION AND COMMAND OF THE LEGION

Diocletian's new legions, such as *II Herculia*, were organized in the same manner as the formations he acquired upon his elevation in AD 284. The legion was composed of ten cohorts (*ILS* 4195 for cohorts X and VII of *II Herculia* in AD 298). There were six centuries in a cohort, each commanded by a centurion with the following titles (ranked according to seniority):

pilus prior
pilus posterior

princeps prior
princeps posterior

hastatus prior
hastatus posterior

These titles harked back to the manipular legions of the middle-Republic (3rd and 2nd centuries BC). In the manipular legion, ten maniples of *hastati* ('spearmen') formed the first battle line, another ten maniples of *principes* ('best men') formed the second line, and a final ten maniples of *triarii* ('third-line men') made up the third line of this *triplex acies* (triple battle line) formation. When the 30 maniples of the legion were grouped into ten cohorts at the end of the 2nd century BC, the maniple was split into two centuries, and so each cohort had two centuries of *hastati*, two of *principes*, and two of *pili* ('javelin men', another title for the *triarii*). The paired centuries were designated *prior* ('front' or 'first') and *posterior* ('rear' or 'following'). The title *posterior* suggests it formed up behind the *prior*, but in his account of the battle of the Sabis (57 BC), Julius Caesar states that he ordered the 'maniples' to open up so the legionaries had room to wield their swords

One of the multi-angular towers at Galerius' fortified palace at Romuliana (Gamzigrad). The palace was built by cohorts I–V of *legio V Macedonica* in the first decade of the 4th century AD, as evidenced by the inscriptions on the bricks used in the construction. (© A. Chen/ISAWNYU)

effectively (*Gallic War* 2.25). If Caesar used maniple to refer to paired centuries, it suggests *priores* and *posteriores* could fight side-by-side.

In Caesar's battle narratives the *triplex acies* was formed by cohorts rather than by lines of *hastati*, *principes* and *pili*. The ten cohorts of the legions assumed a 4-3-3 formation (*Civil War* 1.83), but when Hadrian observed the manoeuvres of *legio III Augusta* at Lambaesis in AD 128, it seems that the centuries of *pili*, *principes* and *hastati* formed up in the old manipular battle lines (Speidel 2006, 28–45).

When Aurelius Iustinus joined *legio XI Claudia* at the close of the 3rd century AD, he was enrolled in the century of a *hastatus posterior* (*ILS* 2332). Dizo, a contemporary of Iustinus in *XI Claudia*, served in the 'first century' (meaning the century of the *pilus prior*) of the sixth cohort (Pais 442). It may be that these ancient centurial titles had lost their tactical significance by *c.* AD 300, but it is interesting to consider that Iustinus may have fought in the first battle line and Dizo in the third. It is unfortunate that the surviving accounts of battles from our era do not go into detail about the composition of battle lines. We do know that Constantine's army deployed initially in *duplex acies* (two battle lines) at Verona (AD 312). The second line appears to have split and formed on the flanks of the first line when the army was threatened with envelopment (*Latin Panegyrics* 12(9).9.1).

The titles of the six centurions of the first cohort were somewhat different. These centurions were known as *ordinarii* (derived from *primi ordines*, 'first rankers'), and were senior to their colleagues in cohorts II–X. Until *c.* AD 260, the most senior centurion of the first cohort, and of the legion as a whole, had been the *primus pilus*, but in our era, the similarly titled *primipilus* or *primipilaris* (previously a status identifying a man who had served as *primus pilus*) referred to civilian supply officers who, like decurions, were often compelled to perform the role.

Following the old *primus pilus* in seniority were the *princeps*, *hastatus*, *pilus posterior*, *princeps posterior* and *hastatus posterior* (*ILS* 2446, *AE*

1993, 1588). The ranks of *princeps* and *hastatus* still existed around AD 300. The Christian martyr Marcellus was *hastatus* of the first cohort of his legion (*Passion of St. Marcellus* (Lanata) 1). As we have seen, Aurelius Gaius served successively as *optio* to a *triarius*, an *ordinarius*, a *princeps*, and was then transferred to the imperial retinue (*AE* 1981, 777). If these centurions were ranked according to seniority, Gaius' final post in the *comitatus* suggests he had exhausted the avenues of promotion within the legion, and that the *princeps* was its most senior centurion.

It is tempting to identify Gaius' *triarius* as one of the *ordinarii*: Vegetius included a *centurio triarius prior* in the first cohort in his reconstruction of the 'ancient legion' (2.8). Vegetius' *triarii* formed a specialist reserve force, who were held behind the legion, ready to counter a successful enemy breakthrough, and were free to perform various manoeuvres without jeopardising the order of the main battle lines (3.14).

The legion was commanded by a *praefectus* (prefect), usually a man who had risen through the ranks and entered the senior officer corps of the *protectores*. Valerius Thiumpus enlisted in *legio XI Claudia* and was transferred to a unit of *lanciarii* attached to the imperial court; proximity to the emperor enabled him to become a *protector*. After five years, Thiumpus was made prefect of *legio II Herculia* (*ILS* 2781).

Legionary tribunes were absent from our era. Divisions and detachments of the legion were commanded by *praepositi*. When legionary tribunes reappear in the third quarter of the 4th century AD, they act as the commanders of the much-reduced legions of the period (e.g. Ammianus Marcellinus 25.6.3).

Lanciarii and Equites Promoti

Lanciarii, soldiers armed with the light *lancia* javelin, formed a large corps within the legion. In AD 299–300, a detachment of *lanciarii* drawn from *legio II Traiana* numbered 439. It was commanded by a *praepositus*, supported by a supernumerary centurion and a standard-bearer (*P.Beatty Panop.* 2.260ff., 286ff; Duncan-Jones 1990). A proportion of legionary *lanciarii* were mounted (*AE* 1981, 777). Legionary *lanciarii* are not to be confused with the *lanciarii* attached to the *comitatus*. As guards units these outranked the legions, but they were in turn junior to the Praetorian Guard which, confusingly, also had *lanciarii* in its ranks (*ILS* 2045, *CIL* VI 2787).

The legions of Diocletian and Constantine had substantial cavalry elements: regular *equites*, mounted *lanciarii* and *equites promoti*. The latter, 'promoted cavalry', were the creation of Diocletian. Detachments of *promoti* were commanded by *praepositi* and subdivided into centuries of uncertain size.

In AD 299, the *equites promoti* of *legio II Traiana* at Tentyra in Egypt numbered 77, very close to the optimum legionary infantry century strength of 80 (Hyginus, *de Munitionibus Castrorum* 1). The pay scale of the *praepositus* of this small detachment reveals him to have been a chief centurion (above). He had at least one centurion under his command (*P.Beatty Panop.* 2.198ff; Duncan-Jones 1990)

In AD 320, the very precisely titled 'vexillation of the *equites promoti* of *legio II Traiana*' was quartered in the Egyptian village of Asphynis. The *praepositus* Decentius was in charge of the detachment and he had at least eight, and perhaps ten or more, centurions under his command. One of the centurions was Valerius Aion. He fell seriously ill and, anticipating death, made a will. The document was witnessed by seven men (the legal requirement), all centurions and described as 'co-colleagues', suggesting they served in the same detachment. Apion, the executor of the will, was another

---

D **COMBAT TECHNIQUES**

A glance at contemporary accounts of the battles of Verona, the Milvian Bridge (AD 312) and Campus Ergenus (AD 313) shows that the essential legionary fighting technique of javelin volley, running charge (*impetus*) into the enemy, followed by toe-to-toe combat with swords, remained the norm, just as it had been centuries before during the time of Julius Caesar **(1)**. It is often supposed that the use of the *spatha* ('long sword') resulted in a change in the Roman sword fighting technique, but that is unlikely. The weapons weren't long by medieval or early modern standards. Like the *gladii* of Republican legionaries, they are best described as medium length, and doubtless continued to be employed in the same general cut-and-thrust manner. Prior to charging to close quarters, the legionary would bombard his enemy with *tela* (javelins), ranging from the small *plumbata* darts **(2)** (the soldiers in the rear ranks of the *centuriae* probably maintained a hail of darts throughout the battle) to long-shanked *pila* and *spicula*, which were thrown at very close range **(3)**. Stones also provided a ready source of ammunition **(4)**. Maxentian soldiers armed with stones are depicted on the siege of Segusium scene on the Arch of Constantine in Rome.

The Hercules blazon on the shield is based on an example on the Arch of Galerius at Thessalonica (dedicated AD 303). The blazon has been supposed to represent *legio II Herculia*, or its off-shoot, the elite *Herculiani* **(5)**. However, Hercules was also an emblem of *legio II Traiana* and, as a symbol of the 'Herculian' branch of the Tetrarchy (i.e. Maximian and his Caesar, Constantius), it might also have been used by guards units.

centurion and presumably Aion's friend and colleague in the *promoti* of *II Traiana*. A tenth centurion is named in the document (he owed Aion money!) and may, again, have been a *promotus* (*P.Col.* 7.188). Did these centurions command regular-sized centuries of 80 men? That seems unlikely. The *promoti* had under-officers called *exarchi* ('overseers') who are thought to have been leaders of sections of six men (Grosse 1920, 124–125). In AD 309, Theodorus, an *exarchus* of the *equites promoti* of *legio III Diocletiana*, was condemned, perhaps because he was a Christian, and his property was confiscated by the state (*Chrest. Mitt.* 196). If the *exarchus* did command a squad of six, it implies the *centuriae* of the *promoti* were composed of multiples of six, whereas infantry *centuriae* had been, and possibly still were, composed of multiples of eight (Hyginus, *de Munitionibus Castrorum* 1; Vegetius 2.7–8 describes sections of ten, reflecting the situation of his day).

Three of the seven witnesses to Aion's will were illiterate and other centurions signed for them. This comes as a shock. Considering their administrative duties and the prominence of written communications, orders and records in the Roman Army, literacy and numeracy should have been essential for centurions (Vegetius 2.19).

The size of the legion

The size of the new legions created by Diocletian and his colleagues is a matter of dispute. In fact, the precise number of legions created in the period AD 284–305 is not known for certain (it is perhaps 17: Campbell 2011). It is often supposed that the new legions were smaller than their early imperial predecessors, but that was not necessarily the case.

The legion of the 1st and 2nd centuries AD was approximately 5,000 men strong (including 120 cavalry), but at least two of Diocletian's new legions, probably *I Iovia* and *II Herculia*, were established with complements of 6,000 (Vegetius, *Epitome* 1.17). The increase in size was partly due to the inclusion of a much enlarged cavalry component. However, it was also needed to facilitate Diocletian's policy of dividing the legions (at least on the Danube frontier) into substantial half-legions of five cohorts apiece. Each half of the legion was placed under a *praepositus* but overall command remained with the prefect (see Christodoulou 2002 for the division and command structure of *legio V Macedonica* in AD 300).

As its name indicates, *legio I Pontica* was established by Diocletian to garrison the Black Sea province of Pontus, and the legion had its headquarters at Trapezus (Trabzon) (*ILS* 639). However, the distribution of the manpower of the legion began immediately after its formation. In AD 288, the prefect of *I Pontica* was overseeing the construction of a fortress and parade ground for a detachment of the legion at Colybrassus in Rough Cilicia, hundreds of miles south-west of Pontus (*AE* 1972, 636). It is not known if *I Pontica* was established at the classic size of *c.*5,000 or the larger strength of 6,000, but other legions, both new creations and pre-Diocletianic formations, must have been substantial. In Egypt in AD 299–300, *III Diocletiana* had more than 1,000 men serving in two vexillations, as did *II Traiana*, and a single detachment drawn from 'Eastern legions' was 998-strong (Duncan-Jones 1990). The numbers are comparable with the milliary (1,000-strong) legionary vexillations of the 2nd and 3rd centuries AD (*ILS* 2726, 531). It is thought that the *milites miliarenses* ('the thousand soldiers') stationed at Syene on the Nile in the early 5th century AD originated as a vexillation of the Syrian legions *III Gallica* and *I Illyricorum*, which was at Coptos in AD 316 and Syene in 321 (*ILS* 8882; *AE* 1909, 29; Brennan 1989, 200).

The new legions established by Diocletian between AD 285, when he eliminated Carinus, and 305, when he abdicated, seem likely to have been similar, and sometimes even greater, in size to the legions raised in previous centuries. However, Diocletian's policy of dividing legions, and the practice of permanently removing large vexillations to provide garrisons for foreign provinces or to create new 'legions' for the imperial field armies (the famous *Ioviani* and *Herculiani* were likely detachments of *I Iovia* and *II Herculia*), ensured that the era of the classic legion of ten cohorts was over.

It is ironic that Diocletian, the conservative guardian of old Roman values and founder of more legions than any emperor since Augustus, immediately broke up his new creations. They would never be reassembled.

ON CAMPAIGN

Constantine's war against Maxentius

The best recorded campaign of the age is Constantine's invasion of Italy in AD 312. The reconstruction here follows two very detailed panegyrics. The first was delivered before Constantine by an anonymous orator at Trier in AD 313 (*Latin Panegyrics* 12(9).2–21). The second, by Nazarius, was delivered to the Senate in Rome in AD 321 (*Latin Panegryics* 4(12).17–32). These long speeches are supplemented by a large body of literary sources, some of which,

Constantine's army on the march into Italy in AD 312. *Cornicines* (horn players) and *signiferi* are followed by infantry and the baggage train. Arch of Constantine (AD 315). (© RHC Archive)

like Lactantius, are contemporary accounts, and a number of inscriptions, mostly from gravestones thought to belong to casualties of the campaign (Ritterling 1924/5, 1474, 1546; Hoffmann 1969, I 258–260).

The capture of Segusium

Constantine's army marched from Gaul in the spring of AD 312. The army was large, a little under 40,000 strong. This represented a quarter of the forces available to the emperor, and the removal of so many men required a careful reorganization of the defences of the Rhine frontier.

Constantine's sudden passage of the Alps into north-west Italy took Maxentius by surprise. The main part of Maxentius' army was located to the east at Verona and Aquileia to meet an anticipated invasion by Licinius. However, Constantine still found his advance blocked by substantial Maxentius forces based at Segusium (Susa) and Augusta Taurinorum (Turin).

Segusium lay at the foot of the Cottian Alps. Its garrison was invited to surrender, but the Maxentians declined and manned the ramparts. Constantine did not waste time on complex siege works and ordered his men to take the fortress by storm. Flaming torches were piled under the gates and ladders were thrown up against the walls. As legionaries and auxiliaries scrambled up the ladders, their comrades provided covering 'fire' with a hail of javelins and sling bullets. Once they gained the ramparts, Constantine's veterans overwhelmed the garrison. The city was ripe for plunder, but the victors instead set about putting out the fires at the gates and reassured the

PRAYER BEFORE THE BATTLE OF CAMPUS ERGENUS, 30 APRIL AD 313

According to the contemporary Christian writer Lactanitus, on the eve of the battle at Campus Ergenus, the emperor Licinius was visited in a dream by an angel. In order to defeat his rival Maximinus Daia, who was a staunch pagan and persecutor of the Christians, the angel told Licinius that he and his whole army:

> must pray to the Supreme God with these words: Supreme God, we beseech Thee; Holy God, we beseech Thee; unto Thee we commend all justice; unto Thee we commend our safety; unto Thee we commend our empire. By Thee we live, by Thee we are victorious and fortunate. Supreme, Holy God, hear our prayers; to Thee we stretch forth our arms. Hearken, Holy, Supreme God.
>
> The emperor awoke, immediately called for a secretary and had written copies of the prayer distributed among his officers, 'who were to teach it to the soldiers under their charge. At this all men took fresh courage, in the confidence that victory had been announced to them from heaven.' The following morning, when the armies advanced across the plain of Ergenus and came into full sight of each other, Licinius ordered his men to halt:
>
> The soldiers of Licinius placed their shields [scuta] on the ground, took off their helmets, and, following the example of their officers [praepositi], stretched forth their hands towards heaven. Then the emperor uttered the prayer, and they all repeated it after him. The enemy, doomed to speedy destruction, heard the murmur of the prayers of their adversaries. And now, the ceremony having been performed three times, the soldiers of Licinius became full of courage, buckled on their helmets again, and picked up their shields … So the two armies drew close; the trumpets gave the signal; the military standards advanced; the troops of Licinius charged [impetus]. But their enemies, panic-struck, could neither draw their swords [gladii] nor yet throw their javelins [tela].
>
> (Lactantius, On the Deaths of the Persecutors 46.10–47.1)

Licinius' 30,000 men proceeded to rout Maximinus' 70,000.

It is not surprising that Licinius claimed to have been visited by a divine being. Constantine did so before the battle of the Milvian Bridge and inspired his troops, and Licinius' legionaries certainly believed in angels, but not of the Christian variety (ILS 8882). Note how Christ is absent from the prayer; Lactantius has given a monotheistic pagan prayer a Christian veneer. The supreme god to whom the Licinians prayed was Sol Invictus – Licinius' favourite deity (ILS 8940).

The siege of Segusium (Susa) or Verona on the Arch of Constantine. The emperor (the oversized defaced figure to the left) directs the assault. Victory hovers behind him, but the Maxentians defend the walls tenaciously with spears and stones. (© D. Entwistle)

Gravestone of Klaudius Ingenuus, a pagan officer of one of Constantine's catafract units (*CIL* XIII 1848). A *calo* follows with Ingenuus' shield and a spare lance. (© A. Fafournoux)

citizens that they came as liberators. Such was the force of Constantine's personality that he could even prevent the usual orgy of rape and destruction that followed the violent capture of a city.

The battle of Turin

With Segusium secured, victorious Constantine advanced on Augusta Taurinorum. Here Maxentius had stationed an army with a large corps of fully armoured heavy cavalry known in soldiers' speech as *clibanarii* ('oven-men'). The unnamed Maxentian general attempted a frontal charge, but Constantine employed what the Romans' called a *forfex* ('forceps') manoeuvre to engulf the flanks of the cavalry. The heavily armoured Maxentians were then beaten from their saddles with iron-reinforced clubs. Those who escaped were pursued to Turin, but the citizens had closed the gates and the fugitives were massacred beneath the city walls.

A gravestone from Eporedia (Ivrea), a little to the north of Turin, commemorates Valerius Ienuarius, a local man who served in a *vexillatio catafractariorum* (*CIL* V 6784). Ienuarius' *vexillatio* was a new-style unit of heavy cavalry and not a legionary detachment. His rank of *circitator* was equivalent to the legionary *tesserarius* (Vegetius 3.8). He was probably one of the Maxentian heavy cavalrymen killed in the battle.

A cluster of gravestones from Turin and Ivrea probably belong to other Maxentiuan casualties of the battle. Aurelius Marcianus was a cavalry *circitor* (*CIL* V 6999). The officer Aurelius Crescentianus, who bore the honorific title *vir egregius* (outstanding man), was 'killed in the battle line'; the gravestone was set up by his brother, an under-officer in a cavalry regiment (*CIL* V 6998). Aurelius Maximus was a 20-year-old *exarchus* of a unit of Dalmatian cavalry; he was commemorated by his friend Aurelius Victorinus, a centurion in one of the legions or Maxentius' Praetorian Guard (*ILS* 2629). Aurelius Senecio, another *exarchus* of the *numerus Dalmatarum*, survived the battle and erected a memorial for his *contubernalis* ('tent' or 'mess mate'), Aurelius Vindex (*CIL* V 7001).

The *numerus* of Maximus and Senecio bore the supplementary title *Divitensium*, indicating that the unit once served at Divitia (Deutz), the bridgehead fort on the Rhine opposite Cologne, probably under Maximian in the AD 280s or 290s. The unit was later attached to Maximian's *comitatus* at Milan and passed to the new emperor Severus in AD 305. When Severus marched against Maxentius and Maximian in spring AD 307, he brought the *numerus* with him but, along with the rest of the field army, it was persuaded to desert to Maxentius, the son of its old commander, Maximian (Lactantius, *On the Deaths of the Persecutors* 26.5, 8–11; Zosimus 2.10).

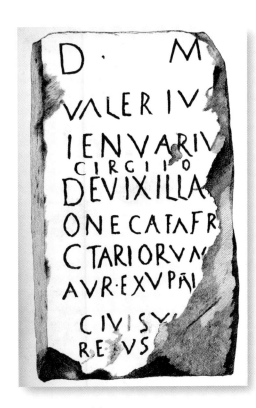

Gravestone of Valerius Ienuarius, *circitor* (officer of the watch) of a Maxentian heavy cavalry unit. He was probably killed at the battle of Turin in AD 312 (*CIL* V 6784). (© RHC Archive)

Maxentius' legionaries

Two centurions of *legio IIII Flavia* were commemorated at Ivrea: 36-year-old Aurelius Vitalis, and a certain Marcus, whose *nomen* and age are lost (*CIL* V 6782, 6783). It is likely that they were killed at Turin, having deserted to Maxentius from the army of Galerius when he invaded Italy in the late summer of AD 307:

Galerius assembled his troops, invaded Italy, and advanced towards Rome, resolving to extinguish the senate and put the whole people to the sword. But he found everything shut and fortified against him. There was no hope of carrying the place by storm, and to besiege it was an arduous undertaking; for Galerius had not brought with him an army sufficient to invest the walls. Having probably never seen Rome, he imagined it to be little superior in size to those cities with which he was acquainted. But some of his legions, detesting the wicked enterprise of a father against his son-in-law [Maxentius was married to Galerius' daughter, Valeria Maximilla], and of Romans against Rome, renounced his authority, and carried over their standards to the enemy. Already had his remaining soldiers begun to waver, when Galerius, dreading a fate like that of Severus, and having his haughty spirit broken and humiliated, threw himself at the feet of his soldiers, and continued to beseech them that he might not be delivered to the foe, until, by the promise of mighty largesses, he prevailed on them. Then he retreated from Rome, and fled in great disorder. He might easily have been cut off in his flight, had any one pursued him even with a small body of troops. He was aware of his danger, and allowed his soldiers to disperse themselves, and to plunder and destroy far and wide, that, if there were any pursuers, they might be deprived of all means of subsistence in a mined country. So the parts of Italy through which that pestilent band took its course were wasted, all things pillaged, matrons forced, virgins violated,

AVRELI . VITALI
CENTVRIONIS . LEG .
IIII . FLA . QVI . VIXIT
ANNOS . XXXVI . PO
SVERVNT . AVRELIVS
PROCEIANVS . CONSO
BRINVS . ET . RESIA . CA
IA . CONIVX . KARISSIMA .

A 16th-century sketch of the gravestone of Aurelius Vitalis, centurion of *legio IIII Flavia* (*CIL* V 6782). He may have deserted Galerius' army in AD 307 and died fighting for Maxentius at Turin in 312. (© RHC Archive)

parents and husbands compelled by torture to disclose where they had concealed their goods, and their wives and daughters; flocks and herds of cattle were driven off like spoils taken from barbarians. And thus did he, once a Roman emperor, but now the ravager of Italy, retire into his own territories, after having afflicted all men indiscriminately with the calamities of war. (Lactantius, *On the Deaths of the Persecutors* 27.2–6)

The gravestone of Aurelius Vitalis is known only from a 16th-century sketch. The artist depicted Vitalis in contemporary plate armour, but the general style of the memorial is typical of our era: the deceased is mounted and followed by his *calo* (Franzoni 1987, no. 64). Vitalis thus appears like a medieval knight, but the inscription does not distinguish him as a centurion of legionary cavalry. Once again, the horse would appear to be a privilege of rank rather than an indicator of the type of troops he led. Vitalis would have fought on foot at Turin, and died in the front rank of his century.

The siege and battle of Verona

The gates of Turin were opened for Constantine. Mediolanum (Milan), suffering from the exactions necessary to maintain Maxentius' large army, soon declared for the liberator. Constantine made his headquarters there and allowed his army to recuperate. In late summer, Constantine moved on the key Maxentian stronghold of Verona. En route, he defeated a large force of cavalry at Brixia (Brescia), and the survivors were hotly pursued the 40 miles to Verona. It is thought that Maxentius's *equites singulares Augusti* (emperor's horse guards) fought at

F THE BATTLE OF TURIN, AD 312

At the battle of Turin in AD 312, Constantine used a *forfex* (forceps) formation to envelop the *cuneus* (wedge formation) of the *clibanarii* ('oven men') heavy cavalry at the centre of the Maxentian battle line. The term *clibanarii* derives from *clibanus* (oven) and was military slang for an armoured rider on a fully armoured horse (bard and chamfron). Constantine's own battle line had heavy cavalry at the centre, but the major source for information about the battle emphasizes that they were *catafractarii*, whose horses were probably unarmoured. Constantine's *catafractarii*, some of whom were probably legionary cavalry, were armed with maces and used these to batter the enemy *clibanarii* to death (*Latin Panegyrics* 12(9).6.2–5, 4(12).23–24).

It is likely that Constantine's infantry also used clubs against the *clibanarii*. This was an occasional Roman infantry tactic. At Singara in AD 343, steely nerved Roman infantrymen faced down charging Persian catafracts, stepping aside at the last possible moment to batter the passing riders from their saddles (Libanius, *Orations* 59.110). In this reconstruction, two of Constantine's legionaries use the same tactic against a Maxentian *clibanarius*. The heads on their maces are modelled after an example from Cibalae (the scene of another battle involving heavy cavalry in AD 316: *Origin of Constantine* 5.16). Their plate armour, the so-called *lorica segementata*, may seem anachronistic, but a growing body of finds from late 3rd- and early 4th-century contexts at Carlisle and León (base of *VII Gemina*; the legion may have supplied a vexillation to Constantine's army), suggest it was still in limited use (Bishop 2013).

Brixia. The gravestone of a cavalryman discovered at Brixia has lost its inscription but bears the typical iconography of the funerary monuments of the Horse Guard at Rome, and its date (end of the 3rd to the start of the 4th century AD) and location combine to suggest a casualty of the cavalry battle at Brixia (Franzoni 1987, no. 49; Speidel 1994, 153).

Protected on three sides by a great loop of the River Adige, Verona proved difficult to place under effective siege. The city was held by Ruricius Pompeianus, Maxentius' resourceful and courageous praetorian prefect. Pompeianus harassed the besiegers with sorties, and then made a daring escape through Constantine's siege lines. He returned with a substantial relief force, presumably gathered from the legionary and cavalry garrisons of north-eastern cities like Aquileia (strong forces had been based in the region to meet an anticipated attack from Licinius). It seemed that the besieger was about to become the besieged, trapped between Verona and Pompeianus' new army, but Constantine emerged triumphant.

The emperor divided his army: he left one part to continue the siege, and led the other across the Adige to do battle with the relief force. Constantine had earned his spurs as a cavalry commander in the Persian and Sarmatian wars of the emperor Galerius and, as night was falling, he led the decisive attack against Pompeianus' apparently larger army. The anonymous panegyrist of AD 313 rebukes Constantine for risking his life, but nonetheless revels in how the emperor 'cut a path through the enemy by slaughter'. Pompeianus was among those slaughtered and his army was routed; Verona surrendered soon after.

Valerius Florentius and Valerius Herodius, from Suasa in Umbria, may have died alongside Pompeianus. The brothers apparently enlisted as guardsmen on the same day and died together, two years and six months later, while serving on the staff of a praetorian prefect (ILS 9075). The brothers were openly Christian, which suggests enlistment in the Praetorian Guard of the pagan but tolerant Maxentius. They may have died on the same day as the result of an accident or epidemic, but it is tempting to see them as casualties of Verona, or the battle of the Milvian Bridge (Seston 1980, 491).

Following the capture of Verona, brief sieges then secured Aquileia and Mutina (Modena) for Constantine. The north of Italy belonged to the emperor, but Maxentius still held Rome. Maxentius had gambled on a successful defence of the north. He had only one army left and it was based at Rome, and so Constantine advanced into peninsular Italy unopposed.

Constantine's legionaries

As professor of rhetoric at Nicomedia, Lactantius was well acquainted with the forces attached to the *comitatus* of Diocletian. He was also well-informed about avenues of promotion in the army, officer grades and new guard units that had superseded the praetorians (*On the Deaths of the Persecutors* 12.5, 19.6, 18.10, 40.5). When Diocletian abdicated in AD 305, Lactantius records how senior representatives from all the legions were invited to the ceremony at Nicomedia (ibid. 19.1). No mention is made of the presence of the commanders of old- or new-style auxiliary regiments. The implication is that after the various imperial guards units, the legionaries remained senior in the pecking order of the Roman Army and represented the backbone of its manpower. The departing emperor, and his successors installed that day, could not risk insulting the legions by excluding them from the ceremony. It is notable that of the forces in the powerful field armies of Galerius in AD 307 and Maximinus in AD 313, Lactantius thought it worthwhile to mention only the legionaries (ibid. 27.3, 47.2). Similarly, when writing *The Origin of Constantine* shortly after the death of the emperor in AD 337, the anonymous author refers only to the 'legions of Constantine' in the final campaign against Licinius in AD 324 (5.28; compare Aurelius Victor 39.42 on the field army of Constantius I in AD 296 being composed of legions). Constantine's army in AD 312 was, therefore, based around a core of legionaries supported by guardsmen, new-style cavalry units (also known as *vexillationes*, cf. *AE* 1937, 232) and contingents levied from recently defeated German tribes (Zosimus 2.15).

Facsimile of a gold medallion showing Constantius I entering London after the defeat and death of Allectus in AD 296. Legionaries formed the core of Constantius' army during the campaign. (© World Imaging)

Zosimus notes that Constantine drew on forces from Britain (2.15). Detachments may then have been sent by the legions *II Augusta*, *VI Victrix* and *XX Valeria Victrix*. Spain's *legio VII Gemina* might also have contributed a vexillation. Constantine's careful reorganization of the Rhine frontier in advance of the campaign (cf. *Latin Panegyrics* 12(9).2.6) points to the five legions of the German provinces contributing the largest contingents: *XXX Ulpia Victrix*, *I Minervia*, *XXII Primigenia*, *VIII Augusta* and *I Martia*. The latter was a very recent creation, being named in honour of the patron deity of Galerius (cp. the *Iovia* and *Herculia* legions named after Diocletian and Maximian).

The men of *legio XXII Primigenia* referred to themselves as *Duoetvicensimani*, 'the Twenty-seconds' and were responsible for the construction of Constantine's new fortress at Divitia in the years between AD 310 and 315 (*ILS* 8937). It is uncertain why the work was undertaken by the legion from Mongontiacum (Mainz) and not *I Minervia*, whose base at Bonna was far closer to Divitia. Bricks from Divitia are stamped *LEG XXII CV* (Hanel & Verstegen 2009). The letters *CV* could refer to the honorific titles *Constantiniana* ('Constantine's own') and *victrix* ('victorious'), demonstrating Constantine's favour and the role the legion played in one of his victories. Another interpretation of *CV* is that, following the brickstamps of *legio V Macedonica* from Romuliana (Christodoulou 2002; *AE* 2002, 1237a1–7), it could refer individually to the fifth cohort, or all five cohorts of a complete half-legion. If a half-legion could be deployed on a construction project far from its base – as occurred at Galerius' palace at Romuliana in the first decade of the 4th century AD – we should perhaps wonder if a half-legion of five cohorts, and not just a vexillation drawn from those cohorts, could fight in a campaign.

Brickstamps of *legio VIII Augusta* bear the abbreviated titles *C ARG* (*AE* 2010, 1064). The latter clearly refers to the legion's headquarters at Argentorate (Strasbourg), while the former is likely to be *Constantiniana*, which hints at valiant service in Constantine's German campaigns or the war of AD 312. Of Constantine's legions, *VIII Augusta* and *I Martia* were located closest to Italy.

The *Divitenses*

We can track the progress of Constantine's advance on Rome in autumn AD 312 by memorials to his soldiers left along the Flaminian Way, the road that led from Umbria to Rome. These soldiers had probably succumbed to wounds sustained in the battles in the north. At Spoletium (Spoleto), a gravestone was erected for Florius Baudio, a 40-year-old veteran with 25 years' service (*ILS* 2777). He died with the rank of *vir ducenarius protector*, having been promoted from the post of *ordinarius* in *legio II Italica*

G   **THE BATTLE OF ADRIANOPLE, AD 324**

A squadron of Constantine's cavalry guard charges across the River Hebrus, surprising an outpost of Licinian legionaries (Zosimus 2.22). The guardsmen carry the *Labarum*, Constantine's Christian battle standard. It follows the style of the old Roman *vexillum*, but is tipped with a *Chi-Rho* symbol (a ligature of the Greek letters *X* and *P* serving as an abbreviation for the name of Christ), and the banner itself is adorned with jewels and portraits of Constantine and his three eldest sons. The *Labarum* was believed to protect its bearer from any danger (Eusebius, *Life of Constantine* 1.29–31, 2.8–9).

The Licinian legionaries are rallied by veteran *signiferi* (standard-bearers). One carries an old-fashioned centurial standard with seven *phalerae* (decorative discs) that is tipped with a *manus* (hand), harking back to the days when the legion was composed of subunits called *manipuli*, 'handfuls' of soldiers. The other standard-bearer carries a *draco* (dragon). Recently borrowed from the cavalry, the *draco* would soon replace the traditional centurial *signum* (standard) and the *signifer* would acquire the title of *draconarius* (Vegetius 2.13). Both standard-bearers wear heavy gold torques on their necks, a typical later Roman decoration for valour.

The shields of Constantine's guardsmen bear the Christian *Chi-Rho* (Lactantius, *On the Deaths of the Persecutors* 44.5). However, the shields of Licinius' legionaries retain traditional legionary badges – eagles and lions. The depiction of eagles and lions on the Arch of Galerius (AD 303) and a winged Victory on the Arch of Constantine (AD 315) indicate that these traditional devices were still in use. It would, therefore, have been appropriate for them to be used by the soldiers of an emperor described as 'a most strict guardian of the military according to the institutes of our forefathers' (*Epitome de Caesaribus* 41.9).

Divitensium. The gravestone was commissioned by his son, Valerius Vario, an *optio* in the same legion.

The headquarters of *legio II Italica* was Lauriacum (Enns) in Noricum, a province in Licinius' domains but, as we have seen, a detachment of the legion had fought in Maximian's African War in AD 297–298 and on returning to Europe it was transferred to Constantius I and quartered at Divitia and assumed the title *Divitensium*.

As a *protector*, 'bodyguard' of the emperor, Baudio was a member of the officer class of the later empire. The title of *vir ducenarius*, borrowed from the old equestrian system, indicated Baudio's seniority: he was two grades above Aurelius Crescentianus, the Maxentian *vir egregius* killed at Turin (*Theodosian Code* 12.1.5).

At Ocriculum (Otricoli), about halfway between Spoletium and Rome, two more soldiers of the *Divitenses* were commemorated. Valerius Iustinus of cohort VII was buried by his father and brother, and Valerius Saturnanus of cohort VI was given a memorial by his brother: for these men the legion really was family (*AE* 1982, 258; *CIL* XI 4085). Finally, the gravestone at Rome of Valerius Genialis, a standard-bearer of the *Divitenses*, suggests that he was killed at the battle of the Milvian Bridge (*ILS* 2346).

Maxentius the leader

On 28 October AD 312, Constantine found Maxentius waiting for him outside Rome. Maxentius could have shut himself behind the mighty walls of Rome. This tactic had worked splendidly in AD 307 when Severus, and then his master, Galerius, attempted to oust the usurper. Their armies quickly became restive when faced with the prospect of trying to surround the 12-mile circuit of the walls.

As we have seen, Severus' army, made up of veteran troops who had previously served Maximian, was induced to desert by bribery. Galerius narrowly managed to extricate himself by appealing to the troops and allowing them to plunder the course of the Flaminian Way (cf. *Origin of Constantine* 3.7; unlike Severus, Galerius retained the support of his lieutenants, including Licinius). However, by AD 312, high taxation and episodes of repression had caused Maxentius' popularity to plummet. Despite the stockpiling of food and other supplies and the heightening of the city walls, the population of Rome would not stand siege. Moreover, the emperor's pride was stung. On learning of Constantine's advance on Rome, the populace rioted and chanted 'Constantine is invincible!' Maxentius was infuriated and desired to legitimize his rule by victory in battle.

Our picture of Maxentius – indolent, deviant and cowardly – owes much to Constantine's propaganda (Aurelius Victor 40.19–20; *Epitome de Caesaribus* 40.13). The anonymous panegyrist of AD 313 claims that Maxentius was too lazy to train with his praetorians and legionaries at

Maxentius. Despite Constantine's propaganda, Maxentius was a competent military leader and retained the loyalty of his troops to the very end. (© Jebulon)

Rome. That is most unlikely. Even Nero, the most unmilitary of Roman princes, found it expedient to show himself a *commilito* (fellow-soldier) by joining in with the exercises of the guardsman on the parade ground (Suetonius, *Nero* 7.2). Despite the successive losses in the north to Constantine, Maxentius was not abandoned by his troops like Severus, nor was he threatened with desertion like Galerius. It is a telling fact that Maxentius could successfully harangue his troops (*Latin Panegyrics* 12(9).14.6). As the son of an Augustus, Maxentius would have been sent to the court of another Tetrarch to learn the arts of leadership. That he remained in power for six years is a testament to his force of personality and charisma. His hold over the troops is revealed by an incident in spring AD 308:

Gilded ridge helmet, with coloured glass ornaments, from Berkasovo. Constantine wore a similar helmet at the battle of the Milvian Bridge, but his was adorned with real gems (*Latin Panegyrics* 4(12).29.5). (© Jebulon)

> Maximian held authority in common with his son, but more obedience was yielded to the young man than to the old. Maxentius had most power and had been longest in possession of it, and it was to him that Maximian owed on this occasion the imperial dignity. The old man was impatient at being denied the exercise of uncontrolled sovereignty, and envied his son with a childish spirit of rivalry. He therefore began to consider how he might expel Maxentius and resume his old dominion. This appeared easy, because the soldiers who deserted Severus had originally served in his own army. He called an assembly of the people of Rome and of the soldiers, as if he had been to make a harangue on the calamitous situation of public affairs. After having spoken much on that subject, he stretched his hands towards his son, charged him as author of all ills and prime cause of the calamities of the state, and then tore the purple robe of state from his shoulders. Thus stripped, Maxentius leaped from the tribunal and was received into the arms of the soldiers. Their rage and clamour confounded the unnatural old man and, like another Tarquin the Proud, he was driven from Rome. (Lactantius, *On the Deaths of the Persecutors* 28)

Sometime later, the temple of Fortuna was destroyed by fire. The disaster was blamed on a soldier (a praetorian?) heard 'uttering blasphemies'. He was lynched by a mob of civilians. Maxentius' soldiers were incensed and went on the rampage. 'They would have destroyed the whole city', wrote Zosimus, 'had not Maxentius promptly quelled their rage' (2.13). Maxentius' ability to quickly bring the soldiers to heel underlines his powers of persuasion.

The battle of the Milvian Bridge
The Milvian Bridge carried the Flaminian Way over the River Tiber just to the north of Rome. The bridge was a mere two miles from the city's Flaminian Gate and Maxentius, having intended to stand siege, dismantled it to slow Constantine's final advance. However, early on 28 October (the sixth

Gilded ridge helmet from Deurne of the type used by Constantine's cavalry officers in the campaign of AD 312.
(© Michiel2005)

anniversary of his elevation by the Praetorian Guard), the last emperor to rule from Rome decided to risk all on pitched battle. Maxentius was no coward and he had a loyal army of veteran troops – praetorians, cavalry guard and legionaries, as well as conscripts from Italy and North Africa. Zosimus suggests that Maxentius' troops outnumbered Constantine's forces by two to one (2.15). That is most unlikely. At the start of the war Maxentius had 100,000 men, probably the total strength of his armies in Italy and North Africa.

Maxentius led his men across a bridge of boats just a little upstream of the Milvian crossing to the area known today as Tor di Quinto. It was a strong position, his left flank protected by steeply rising bluffs and his right by the Tiber. There was no room on this ground formed by a meander of the river for fancy tactics or manoeuvres. It would be a head-on clash, but the river also curved behind Maxentius' position: he had no easy line of retreat.

The battle of the Milvian Bridge was hard fought, but Maxentius' choice of battleground was his undoing. His cavalry and then infantry were gradually forced towards the river; the prospect of death by drowning caused panic. Maxentius' troops broke and fled for the bridge of boats, but the Praetorian Guard stood firm, covering the retreat of the emperor it had made. The Guard had been greatly understrength in AD 306 but Maxentius replenished its ten cohorts from the legionaries who deserted Severus and Galerius in AD 307 (e.g. *CIL* VI 37207, *ILS* 2041). The panegyrist of AD 313 tells us, with some admiration, that these warriors

H   LEGIONARY COMMANDER, AD 337

By the time Constantine died in AD 337, the legions had fragmented into frontier and field army units of varying size. Only the half-legions on the Danube frontier bore any resemblance to the classic legion, and these must have been diminished by detachments. The mini-legions in the now permanent imperial and regional field armies (*comitatenses*, from *comitatus*, 'court') outranked the frontier legions (*ripenses*, 'river bank' units) (*Theodosian Code* 7.20.4). Prefects remained in charge of the various elements of the frontier legions, but field army legions were commanded by tribunes (Ammianus Marcellinus 25.6.3). Here we see such an officer, distinguished by his finely dyed and embroidered clothing and a gilded and jewelled ridge helmet (**1**) (see inset for variants of the type and method of construction (**2**)). The tribune's richly decorated sword, scabbard and belt follow examples from the grave of a Roman officer at Durostorum. The officer was buried with a second sword, with a shorter and narrower blade for thrusting (**3**), highlighting, once again, that the popular notion of later Roman soldiers using long, slashing swords should be treated with caution (Dumanov 2005).

The Tetrarchs and their successors maintained the close-cropped hair favoured by soldiers and stubble on their faces symbolized how they were constantly fighting or labouring on behalf of the Empire and had no time to shave. Constantine followed this fashion for a time, but he then affected a hairstyle and clean-shaven look modelled after the portraiture of the first emperor, Augustus. Towards the end of his reign, Constantine adopted a longer hairstyle, which was of course imitated by his subjects, including this tribune.

In AD 312, the Milvian Bridge was located a short distance to the north of Rome. However, the area where Constantine defeated Maxentius is now covered by the sprawl of the modern city. (© P. Ferri)

'covered with their bodies the place they had chosen for combat', but it was for nothing. Constantine, at the head of his cavalry guard and conspicuous in his gem-encrusted helmet and gilded shield, pressed his attack and broke through the thinned ranks of the praetorians. Maxentius and his cavalry guard attempted to cross the bridge of boats, but it was already overloaded with fugitives and collapsed. Maxentius was dragged under by the weight of his armour, and thousands of his soldiers drowned (Zosimus 2.16; *Epitome de Caesaribus* 40.7).

Maxentius' corpse, identified by its rich imperial garments and splendid armour, was pulled from the Tiber on 29 October. The head of the 'tyrant' was hacked off and impaled on a spear. Constantine then entered Rome in triumph, but the liberator bypassed the Capitol and so avoided the customary sacrifice to Jupiter, the principal god of the Roman state. Why? Constantine was convinced his victory was inspired by the god of the Christians.

The dream

Writing soon after the event, Lactantius reveals that on the eve of battle Constantine was 'advised in a dream to mark the heavenly sign of God on the shields of his soldiers and then engage in battle'. The heavenly sign was probably the '*Chi-Rho*' monogram – a combination of the Greek letters X (*chi*) and P (*rho*) that served as an abbreviation of Christ.

The dream has become conflated with Constantine's vision of Christ and the Cross. This vision, apparently shared by his field army sometime in

SIC·XX

advance of the campaign of 312 (perhaps two years earlier), only became common knowledge after it was revealed by the emperor to his biographer, the bishop Eusebius of Caesarea, probably in AD 336. It was the dream recounted by Lactantius, doubtless confirmed as coming from God by the Christian bishops in Constantine's retinue, and the resulting victory at the Milvian Bridge, that ensured the emperor's public conversion to Christianity.

Of the Christian accounts of the battle, Lactantius' *On the Deaths of the Persecutors* 44, is crucial for the description of Constantine's dream about marking the 'heavenly sign of God' on his soldiers' shields, but Eusebius' *Ecclesiastical History* makes no mention of it (9.9.3–11). Eusebius' *Life of Constantine*, published after the emperor's death in AD 337, introduces the famous vision of Christ and the Cross and the dream that inspired Constantine to create the *labarum* battle standard (1.27–32; for the battle, 1.37–38). It may be that Constantine's vision of Christ and the Cross was a reinterpretation of a vision he had in *c.* AD 310 involving the sun god Apollo (*Latin Panegyrics* 6(7).21.4). It may be that Apollo/Sol, a favourite of pagan monotheists and Constantine's patron deity prior to his conversion, was subsequently assimilated with Christ in the mind of the emperor.

The battle of the Milvian Bridge on the Arch of Constantine. Maxentius and his cavalry guard (in the scale armour typical of guardsmen) tumble into the swirling waters of the Tiber. To the right, a *tubicen* (trumpeter) and *cornicen* (horn player) drive on Constantine's cavalry. (© Autumnal Fires)

BATTLE

Battle formations

At the battle of Turin (AD 312), the Maxentian army formed up on a hill in a *cuneus* (wedge) formation. *Clibanarii* were at the point and the infantry were on the wings, but mostly concealed behind the hill. The Maxentian general (he is not named) planned to swing the wings of infantry forward and envelop Constantine's army, but the emperor deduced the stratagem and countered with a *forfex* (forceps) manoeuvre. The wings of Constantine's V-shaped formation engaged first and surrounded the flanks of the Maxentian army. The emperor, positioned at the centre of the battle line with his own heavy cavalry, charged into the *clibanarii* and completed the rout (*Latin Panegyrics* 12(9).6.2–5, 4(12).23–24). Nazarius tells us that Constantine's catafracts were trained to charge like battering rams and that they invariably crashed through the enemy (ibid. 4(12).23.4). The principal weapon of the catafract was the *contus* (heavy lance). Some legionary cavalry were equipped with the *contus* (*P.Col.* 7.188), and it can be assumed that some of the men who followed Constantine in that charge were legionary *equites*.

In the following battle at Verona, Constantine employed a typical linear battle line. It was a double line (*duplex acies*), but when threatened with envelopment by the larger force of Pompeianus, the emperor reduced the depth of his army and formed it into a longer, single line (*simplex acies*). Constantine believed the *animus* (spirit) of his men would prevent the Maxentians from breaking through. He was right. Inspired by their emperor's display of *virtus* (valour) – Constantine was, as usual, fighting at the head of his cavalry guard – the legionary infantry won the close quarter combat with *tela* (javelins) and *gladii* (swords), and annihilated the enemy (*Latin Panegyrics* 12(9).9–10).

The emperor Maximinus was the nephew of Galerius and he bitterly resented the elevation of Licinius, Galerius' old friend and comrade, to the rank of senior emperor in AD 308. In AD 313, Maximinus invaded Licinius' province of Thrace and captured Byzantium and Heraclea, but he panicked during the battle of Campus Ergenus and fled, causing the *animus* of his legions to collapse. (© RHC Archive)

Morale

At the Milvian Bridge, the final battle of the campaign, the *animus* of Maxentius' Italian and North African levies was low, but the spirit of his legionaries, praetorians and cavalry guard was high. Like Constantine's army, Maxentius' (apparently) huge force was arrayed with infantry at the centre and cavalry on the flanks. His army was probably arrayed in two or more lines with reserves (*subsidia*) to the rear. The cavalry opened the battle, and Constantine's men were victorious. The infantry then charged (*impetus*) and Maxentius' untried levies broke but Maxentius' cavalry guard, the legionaries who had deserted to him from the field armies of Severus and Galerius, and the Praetorian Guard (brought up to strength by transfers from the same legionary forces), put up a fierce resistance. However, even their *animus* could not hold back Constantine (again leading from the front), and they left an unbroken line of dead along the bank of the River Tiber (*Latin Panegyrics* 4(12).30.1; Zosimus 2.16).

No fancy tactics were employed at the battle of the Milvian Bridge. It was a

The emperor Licinius was a competent general, and he skilfully outmanoeuvred Constantine at Beroea in AD 317 (*Origin of Constantine* 5.18). However, he lacked Constantine's charisma and steadfastness and was not averse to abandoning his armies in order to save himself. (© RHC Archive)

purely frontal battle: Constantine and his men charged forward and Maxentius' men resisted. Maxentius hoped his choice of battle ground, with the River Tiber immediately to the rear giving no means of escape, would force all of his men to stand their ground, but it merely encouraged the new levies to panic.

The battle of Campus Ergenus (located between Edirne and Marmara Ereğlisi) was another simple, frontal affair (AD 313). Lactantius' account focuses on the legionary forces forming the main strength of the opposing armies. Despite being outnumbered by more than two to one, the *animus* of Licinius' men was high. After praying to Sol for victory, they hurled their *tela*, suddenly charged forward and hacked into the ranks of Maximinus' legions with their swords. However, victory did not come easily. Maximinus' legionaries stubbornly held their ground and the battle would have ended in a draw if the emperor had not panicked and fled the field. This caused the morale of his army to collapse. Legionaries forgot about their reputations for *virtus* and the *praemia* (rewards) they had earned for brave deeds (*On the Deaths of the Persecutors* 46–47).

Three years later, at Cibalae (Vinkovci), the battle between Constantine and Licinius was set to be a draw, but on seeing their emperor mounted on a horse and ready to flee, Licinius' men became demoralized and retreated, handing the victory to Constantine (Zosimus 2.18). At Chrysopolis (Üsküdar) in AD 324, Licinius' declaration that he would fight alongside his men temporarily heartened his soldiers (Zosimus 2.26), but they suffered massive casualties and surrendered when Constantine's army was reinforced by fresh legionary contingents (*Origin of Constantine* 5.28).

AFTER THE BATTLE

Fought with javelins, swords, lances, clubs, maces and axes, Roman battles were brutal and bloody affairs. Constantine emerged from the frenzied fighting at Verona covered in the blood of the Maxentians he had killed, but this did not deter his generals and senior officers from embracing him and grasping his bloody hands (*Latin Panegyrics* 12(9).10.3; 4(12).26.4). In battles where the defeated had no easy line of retreat, or where they were surrounded, there could be a huge number of casualties. The defeats of the Maxentians at Turin and the Milvian Bridges were almost total. Massacres of fugitives occurred beneath the walls of Turin (the citizens, realizing Constantine was victorious, promptly changed their

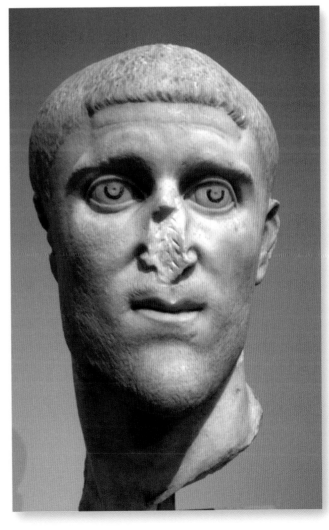

Constantius I famously routed the Alamanni at Lingones in AD 302, but he was actually defeated in the initial skirmish, wounded and pursued. The gates of Lingones were shut and Constantius was hauled up onto the battlements by ropes (Eutropius 10.23). (© Capillon)

Coin issued by Constantine to celebrate his triumphs over the Sarmatians in AD 323. The reverse shows Victory bearing a trophy with a bound Sarmatian captive at her feet. After the battle of Bononia, Constantine forced Sarmatian captives under the yoke and then gave them to his soldiers as slaves. (© RHC Archive)

allegiance and barred the gates), while the bank of the Tiber was lined with heaps of dead, and the river itself was clogged with bodies (ibid. 12(9).6.5, 17.3; 4(12).23.4–5, 30.1). At Verona, the Maxentians who surrendered were treated leniently; they were disarmed and imprisoned for a short time (ibid. 12(9).11.4). Most were probably enrolled into Constantine's army. In five hours of battle and pursuit at Lingones (Langres) (AD 302), the army of Constantius I slaughtered 60,000 Alamanni. The number of casualties is greatly exaggerated, but is indicative of the scale of the defeat (Eutropius 9.23). Vindonissa (Windisch) was the location of another of Constantius' great victories over German invaders (AD 303). The enemy dead were left unburied and heaps of bones were still to be seen years later (*Latin Panegyrics* 6(7).6.3). After surprising the Sarmatians at Campona (Nagyteteny) in AD 323, Constantine left the place 'dripping with blood' and the Danube was filled with corpses (Zosimus 2.21; Porfyrius 6.19–21).

Following victory, the bodies of the dead and the enemy camp were plundered, but Roman soldiers did not always realize the value of what they found. When Galerius' men plundered the camp of the Persian king Narses (AD 298), 'a common soldier, after finding a Parthian [sic] jewel-case full of pearls, threw the gems away in ignorance of their value, and went away content with the mere beauty of his bit of leather' (Ammianus Marcellinus 22.4.8). After the battle of Bononia, the last engagement of Constantine's Sarmatian war of AD 323, the emperor held a parade, humiliated his captives by making them pass under a yoke, and then distributed them as slaves to the assembled soldiers (Porfyrius 6.26–28). Military decorations like torques and special donatives were probably granted by the emperor at parades of the type held at Bononia (Banostor). Compare Josephus, *Jewish War* 7.13–16 and Ammianus Marcellinus 24.6.15 for the distribution of military decorations at similar ceremonies after the capture of Jerusalem (AD 70) and the battle of Ctesiphon (AD 363).

High-ranking captives, like the wife, sisters and children of Narses, were treated with the utmost respect because of their diplomatic value; the

Persian king ceded a considerable amount of territory to secure their return (Petrus Patricius frags 13–14). Other captives were retained for occasional triumphal processions in Rome, but a Frankish or Alamannic king captured by Constantine was more likely to be thrown to the beasts in the arena at Trier for the entertainment of the troops (*Latin Panegyrics* 6(7).10; Eutropius 10.3).

Constantine's triumphal entry into Rome in AD 312, as depicted on the Arch of Constantine. Victory drives the emperor's carriage and a *torquatus* (top centre) looks on. *Torquati* were valiant legionaries who had been decorated with a gold neck torque. They also received double pay and rations. (© R. Martel)

FURTHER READING

Websites

Most of the Latin inscriptions referred to above (*AE, CIL, ILS, Insrc. Aquil.*, Pais), and links to photographs of many, can be found on the Epigraphik-Datenbank Clauss/Slaby: http://db.edcs.eu/epigr/epi_en.php

A podcast of Dr M. C. Bishop's 2013 Caerleon lecture about *lorica segementata* and its survival into the early 4th century AD, can be downloaded from the Internet archive: http://archive.org/details/CaerleonLecture

References

Adams, J. N., & Brennan, P. M., 'The Text at Lactantius, *De Mortibus Persecutorum* 44.2, and Some Epigraphic Evidence for Italian Recruits', *Zeitschrift für Papyrologie und Epigrafik* 84 (1990), pp.183–186

Barnes, T. D., 'Emperors, Panegyrics, Prefects, Provinces and Palaces (284–317)', *Journal of Roman Archaeology* 91 (1996), pp.532–552

Bell, H.I., et al., The Abinnaeus Archive: Papers of a Roman Officer in the Reign of Constantius II, Oxford (1962)

Barnes, T. D., *Constantine: Dynasty, Religion and Power in the Later Roman Empire*, Oxford (2014)

Bishop, M. C., '*Lorica Segmentata*: The Roman Spitfire?', Caerleon Annual Birthday Lecture (2013). See online resources

Brennan, P., 'Diocletian and Elephantine: A Closer Look at Pococke's Puzzle (IGRR 1.1291 = SB 5.8399)', *Zeitschrift für Papyrologie und Epigraphik* 76 (1989), pp.193–205

Campbell, D. B., 'Did Diocletian Overhaul the Roman Army?', *Ancient Warfare* 5.4 (2011), pp.47–52

Christodoulou, D. N., 'Galerius, Gamzigrad and the Fifth Macedonian Legion', *Journal of Roman Archaeology* 15 (2002), pp.275–281

Colombo, M., 'Correzioni testuali ed esegetiche all'epigrafe di Aurelius Gaius (regione di Kotiaeum in 'Phrygia')', *Zeitschrift für Papyrologie und Epigraphik* 174 (2010), pp.118–126

Cowan, R., *Roman Legionary, AD 69–161*, Oxford (2013)

Crawford, M. H., & Reynolds, J. M., 'The Aezani Copy of the Prices Edict', *Zeitschrift für Papyrologie und Epigraphik* 34 (1979), pp.163–210

Drew-Bear, T., 'Les voyages d'Aurélius Gaius, soldat de Dioclétien', in *La géographie administrative et politique d'Alexandre à Mahomet*, Leiden (1981), pp.93–141

Dumanov, B., 'The Encrusted *Spatha* from Durostorum', *Studia Archaelogica Universitatis Serdicensis. Stephanos Archaeologicos in Honorem Professoris Ludmili Getov*, Supplement 4 (2005), pp.310–323

Duncan-Jones, R. P., 'Pay and Numbers in Diocletian's Army' in *Structure and Scale in the Roman Economy*, Cambridge (1990), pp.105–117

Franzoni, C., *Habitus atque Habitudo Militis*, Rome (1987)

Grosse, R., *Römische Militärgeschichte von Gallienus bis zum Beginn der byzantinischen Themenverfassung*, Berlin (1920)

Hoffmann, D., *Das spätrömische Bewegungsheer und die Notitia Dignitatum*, Düsseldorf (1969)

Jones, A. H. M., *The Later Roman Empire 284–602*, Oxford (1964)

Hanel, N., & Verstegen, U., 'The Bridgehead Fort at Cologne-Deutz (Divitia) on the right bank of the Rhine' in *LIMES XX*, Madrid (2009), pp.749–756.

Rance, P., '*Campidoctores, Vicarii vel Tribuni*: The Senior Regimental Officers in the Late Roman Army and the Rise of the *Campidoctor*' in Lewin, A. S. & Pellegrini, P. (eds), *The Late Roman Army in the Near East from Diocletian to the Arab Conquest*, Oxford (2007), pp.395–409

Rea, J. R., *et al.*, 'A Ration-Warrant for an *Adiutor Memoriae*', *Yale Classical Studies* 28 (1985), pp.101–113

Ritterling, E., '*Legio*', *Realencyclopädie der classischen Altertumswissenschaft* 12 (1924/5), pp.1,211–1,829

Seston, W., *Scripta Varia*, Rome (1980)

Speidel, M. A., 'Roman Army Pay Scales', *Journal of Roman Studies* 82 (1992), pp.87–106

Speidel, M. P., *Riding for Caesar*, Cambridge, Mass. (1994)

Speidel, M. P., *Emperor Hadrian's Speeches to the African Armies – A New Text*, Mainz (2006)

Tomlin, R., 'The Owners of the Beaurains (Arras) Treasure' in E. Hartley, *et al.* (eds), *Constantine the Great: York's Roman Emperor*, York (2006), pp.59–64

GLOSSARY

Adiutrix	'Supportive', legion title
animus	spirit, morale
aquila	eagle standard of the legion
aquilifer	eagle-bearer
armatura	advanced weapons drill, also title of instructor of the drill
Augusta	'Augustan', 'of Augustus', legion title derived from the name of the emperor Augustus (27 BC – AD 14)
balteus	military belt
calo	soldier's servant
campidoctor	senior training instructor
centuria	century, tactical subunit of the legion, optimally comprising 80 men
centurio	centurion, commander of *centuria*
circitor	cavalry rank equivalent to *tesserarius*
Claudia	'of Claudius', 'Claudian', legion title derived from the name of the emperor Claudius (AD 41–54)
clibanarius	'oven man', military slang for fully armoured (rider and horse) cavalry
cohors	cohort, legionary unit of six centuries
comitatus	imperial court, retinue (from *comes*, companion of the emperor)
contus	heavy lance
duplicarius	soldier on double pay
eques	cavalryman
equites promoti	'promoted cavalry'
exarchus	'overseer', cavalry under-officer in charge of six troopers
exercitator	senior training officer
Flavia	'Flavian', legion title. The old *legio IIII Flavia* derived its title from the family name of the emperor Vespasian (AD 69–79). The new Tetrarchic legion II *Flavia Constantia* was named after the emperor Flavius Constantius (AD 293–306).
Gemina	'Twin', title indicating a legion originally formed by amalgamation
gladius	sword
hastatus	centurion rank and centurial title
Herculia	'of Hercules', 'Herculean', legion title derived from the patron deity of the emperor Maximian
immunis	soldier exempted from basic and menial duties (munera)
Iovia	'of Jupiter', legion title derived from the patron deity of the emperor Diocletian
Italica	'Italian', legion title
lanciarius	specialist fighter equipped with the *lancia* javelin
legio	legion
lorica	armour
Macedonica	'Macedonian', legion title
magister equitum	'master of cavalry', training officer of legionary cavalry
miles	soldier
Martia	'of Mars', legion title derived from the patron deity of the emperor Galerius

Minervia	'of [the goddess] Minerva', legion title
numerus	unit or regiment
optio	centurion's deputy
ordinarius	senior centurion of the first cohort
Parthica	'Parthian', legion title
pilum	traditional legionary javelin with a long iron shank
plumbata	lead-weighted dart
praepositus	commander of a legionary division or detachment
praefectus	prefect, commanding officer of legion
Primigenia	'first born', legion title
princeps	'foremost', centurial rank and title
principalis	enior under-officer
prior	'front' or 'leading', centurial title
probatus	approved for military service
posterior	'rear' or 'following', centurial title
protector	'bodyguard', title of corps of senior officers
scutum	curved legionary shield
sesquiplicarius	soldier receiving pay-and-a-half
signifer	standard-bearer
spatha	medium-length or long sword
stipendium	military pay, also a term used to denote a year of military service
telum	javelin
tesserarius	officer of the watchword
torquatus	legionary decorated with a torque for valour
Traiana	'of Trajan', legion title derived from the name of the emperor Trajan (AD 98–117)
Valeria	'Valiant', legion title
vexillatio	Legionary detachment, also refers to new variety of cavalry regiments
Victrix	'Victorious', legion title
vitis	the centurion's vine-wood stick, insignia of his rank

INDEX

References to illustrations are shown in **bold**

Abinnaeus, Flavius 14
Adrianople, battle of (AD 324) **49** (48)
Aion, Valerius 16, 36, 38
Ammianus Marcellinus 27, 58
animus 56–57
Aquileia 9–10
aquiliferi **22**
Arch of Constantine **22**, **39**, **42**, 55, 59
Arch of Galerius **11**, **22**, **23**
armatura 26
Aulucentius, Valerius 9, 17, **17**

battle lines/formations **25** (24), 33–34, **45** (44), 55–57
battles, aftermath 57–59
Baudio, Florius 8, 10, 11, 48, 50
Bonitus the Frank 10, 28
Bononia, battle of (AD 323) 58
Brixia (Brescia) 44, 46

Caesar, Julius 27, 33–34
calones 31–32
campidoctores 26–28
Campona (Nagyteteny) 58
Campus Ergenus, battle of (AD 313) **41** (40), 57
Carinus, emperor **18**, 19
Carpi 6, 20, 21
Castus, Valerius 22–23
casualties of battle 57–58
catafracts **45** (44), 56
cavalry **13** (12), **28**
    in battle **45** (44), **49** (48), 52, 54, 55, 56
    horses **13** (12), 17, 28, 30, 44, **45** (44)
    organisation of 36, 38, 42
    ranks 17, 18, 30
    training 28, 30
    weapons **13** (12), **28**, 31
cavalry instructors 28, 30
Christianity 20–22, 24, 26, **41** (40), 54–55
clibanarii **45** (44), 55–56
combat techniques **37** (36)
commanders 35–36, 38, **53** (52)
compulsory military service 11
Constantine
    aftermath of battle 57–59
    Arch of **22**, **39**, **42**, 55, 59
    and Christianity 24, 26, 54–55
    and Cibalae (Vinkovci) 57
    coins of 6, 24, 26
    entry into Rome 59
    his legionaries 47–48, **49** (48)
    and Milvian Bridge 51–52, 54, 55, 56–57
    and organisation of army 4, 34, 36
    and Segusium 40, 42, **42**
    and Turin 42–43, 55–56
    and Verona 44, 46–47, 56, 57
    warrior ethos 28
    wars against Maxentius 39–57
Constantius I 5–6, 20, 24, 47, 57, 58
Crescentianus, Aurelius 42–43
cuneus formation 55

decurions 11
Diocletian **4**, **14**, 46
    abdication of 21
    campaigns 19–20
    and organisation of army 33, 36, 38–39
    and paganism 20–21
    and pay of legionaries 16
Divitenses 48, 50
Divitia (Deutz) 43, 48, 50
Dizo, Aurelius 9, 20
donatives 14–15, **15–16**, 21

eagle-bearers **22**
equipment 31–33
    banners **11**, **49** (48)
    belts 31, **53** (52)
    dracones **11**, **49** (48)
    helmets **13** (12), **18**, **19**, **25** (24), 26, **32**, **37** (36), **45** (44), **51**, **53** (52)
    lorica (armour) **13** (12), **32**, **32**, **33**, **37** (36), **45** (44)

scutum (shield) **9**, **23**, **32**, **32**, **37** (36), **49** (48)
    standards **24**, **25** (24), 26, 31, **49** (48), 55
    see also weapons
equites promoti 36, 38
exarchi 38
exercitator equitum 28, 30
Extricatus, Geminius 30

Flaminian Way 48, 50
Flavinus, Aurelius 10, 16, 17
Florentius, Valerius 46–47
forfex manoeuvre 42, **45** (44), 56
formations
    for battle **25** (24), 33–34, **45** (44), 55–57
    of legions 33–38
frumentarii 23

Gaius, Aurelius 16, 18–22, 35
Galerius **14**, 46
    Arch of **11**, **22**, **23**
    chronology 5–7
    in Egypt 20
    invasion of Italy 43–44, 50
    origins of 10
    palace of **28**, **34**, **35**, 48
    and religion 21, 24
Genialis, Valerius 8, 14, 50
geographical origins of legions 9–10

Hadrian, emperor 30
hastatus 33–34, 34–35
Hercules **22**, 24, **37** (36)
Herodius, Valerius 46–47
horses **13** (12), 17, 28, 30, 44, **45** (44)

Ienuarius, Valerius 42, **43**
Italy, invasions of 6–7, 39–59
Iulius 8, 17, 30
Iustinus, Aurelius 8, **8**, 12, 16, 30, 34
Iustinianus, Claudius 9
Iustinus, Valerius 8, 50

labarum standard **24**, 26, **49** (48), 55
Lactantius **41** (40), 43–44, 47, 51, 54–55, 57
lanicarii **13** (12), 18, 36
Lepontius 31, **32**
Licinius, emperor 10, 24, **41** (40), **49** (48), 56, 57
Longinianus, Valerius 9, 17

magister kampi 30
Marcellus (Christian martyr) 22, 35
Master of Cavalry 28, 30
Maxentius **7**, 50
    and Constantine 39–57
    as a leader 50–51
    his legionaries 43–44
    and Milvian Bridge 51–52, 54, **55**, 56–57
    and Turin 55–56
    and Verona 44, 46–47, 58
Maximian 4–6, 5, 10–11, **14**, 20, 22, 24, 43, 51
Maximianus, Aurelius 9, 10
Maximinus, emperor 6–7, **14**, **41** (40), 46, 56, 57
Milvian Bridge, battle of (AD 312) 51–52, 54, **54**, 55, 56–57
Mithras 23, 24

Narses I of Persia 58–59

organisation of legions 33–39

paganism 20–21, 22–24, 26
pay 9, 14–16, 21
pilus 33–34
Pompeianus, Ruricius 46, 56
praefectus 35
praepositi 35–36
Praetorian Guard 30, 52, 54
primus pilus 34
princeps 33–34, 34–35
Proculinus, Aelius 28, 30
promotion 16–17, 18

ranks 16–17, 18, 30, 33–35

rations 14, 15, 21
recruitment to legions 8–11
roman legions
    I Adiutrix 9, 10, 12
    I Iovia 18, 21, 22, 38, 39
    I Italica 8, 18, 19, 20
    I Martia 47, 48
    I Minervia 8, 20, 24, 47, 48
    I Pontica 38
    II Adiutrix 9, 23, 24, 26, 28, 30
    II Flavia Constantia 15
    II Herculia 11, 16, 20, **23**, 24, 33, 35, 38, 39
    II Italica 8, 11, 14, 20, 31, 48, 50
    II Parthica 12
    II Traiana 15–16, 22, 36, 38
    III Augusta 12, 18, 20, 23, 30, 34
    III Diocletiana 38
    III Italica 20
    IIII Flavia 11, 23, 43, **44**
    IV Flavia 20
    V Macedonica 10, **34**, **35**, 48
    VII Claudia 10, 20
    VII Gemina 47
    VIII Augusta 18, 20, 31, **32**, 47, 48
    X Gemina 10
    XI Claudia 8, 9, **9**, 10, 17, 20, 30, 34, 35
    XV Apollinaris 27
    XX Valeria Victrix 47
    XXII Primigenia 47–48
    XXX Ulpia Victrix 47
Rome 50–52, 54, **54**, 59

Sarmatians 4–7, 19, 21, 28, 30, 58, **58**
Segusium (Susa), siege of 40, 42, **42**
Severus, emperor 6, 43, 50
signiferi (standard-bearers) **25** (24), **39**, **49** (48)
signum **25** (24), **49** (48)
size of legions 38–39
social origins of legionaries 10–11
Sol Invictus 24, 26
Spoletium (Spoleto) 48
Sudlecentius, Aurelius 9, **9**

Tetrarchs, statue of **14**
Thiumpus, Valerius 35, **35**
Thracians 9–10
Tiber, River 51–52, 54, **54**, 56–57, 58
training **25** (24), 26–30
Turin, battle of (AD 312) 42–43, **45** (44), 55–56, 57–58

Vegetius 35
Verona, siege and battle of (AD 312) 34, 44, 46–47, 56, 57, 58
veteran privileges 12, 14
vexillationes 42, 47
Vindonissa (Windisch) 58
Vitalis, Aurelius 43, 44, **44**

warrior ethos 27–28
weapons
    butt-spikes **29** (28)
    clubs 31, **45** (44)
    contus (heavy lance) 31, 56
    gladius (sword) **9**, **13** (12), **29** (28), 30, 31, **53** (52), 56
    hasta (spear) 31
    knives **13** (12)
    lanciae (javelins) **13** (12), 31, 36
    maces 31, **45** (44)
    pila (javelins) **29** (28), **37** (36)
    plumbatae (darts) 31, **31**, **37** (36)
    pugio (daggers) **13** (12)
    scabbards **13** (12), 30, **53** (52)
    spatha (long sword) **9**, **29** (28), 31, **37** (36)
    spicula **29** (28), **37** (36)
    stones **37** (36)
    tela (javelins) **9**, 31, **37** (36), 56
    training in 26–27
    see also equipment

Zosimus 47, 51, 52